C000083095

Social Equations:

The Formulas of Deep Friendships, Charm, Trust, and Being a People Person

By Patrick King
Social Interaction and Conversation Coach at
www.PatrickKingConsulting.com

Table of Contents

5

Chapter 1: You Can't Make a Second First Impression

If you've picked up this book, chances are that you don't consider yourself a naturally social person. Perhaps you see others around you easily and confidently doing things that you find confusing, nerve-wracking, or just a little mysterious. Each of us can probably call to mind a person we've met who seems to socialize and connect with others seamlessly. They come across as likeable, comfortable in themselves, and genuinely witty and charming.

You'd be forgiven for assuming that this kind of social aptitude is inborn—something you either have or you don't have. I'm here to tell you that social skills are not a rare kind of genius that only a select few are capable of. Rather, being able to communicate, to connect, to have fascinating conversations, and to genuinely thrive in social situations is a skill set that depends on a predictable set of rules and principles. There's no magic or luck here! Understand these rules and principles and practice them consistently, and there's no reason *you* cannot be that quintessential social butterfly.

In the chapters that follow, we'll be taking a step-by-step look at some of these core skills and breaking them down in such a way that you can get started mastering them no matter who you are or what your particular limitations are. I've condensed plenty of research and information from a wide range of sources, from experts who study human communication, language, and communication, to psychologists, coaches, and masters of conflict resolution.

Think of the book that follows as a kind of modern-day etiquette book. I know "etiquette" is a disastrously old-fashioned word and may conjure up images of high-collared Victorian repression. In reality, etiquette is about much more than manners and propriety. According to Lynn Coady, we should not "confuse traditional behaviors with good manners. The definition of etiquette is gender neutral—it simply means we strive at all times to ensure a person in our company feels at ease."

To follow the unspoken rules of social behavior means to be aware of yourself and others, to be respectful and considerate, to be adaptable and easy-going, and to always prioritize connection and harmony over everything else. This book may be a little different from others you may have read on the subject; we will be exploring not just the unspoken rules of good conversation and the mysterious ins and outs of forming friendships, but also the less appreciated skills, such as how and when to say no, when to keep quiet, and how to earn someone's trust.

There's a little of everything here, and you'll find that the principles we cover will apply to professional and personal relationships, to casual and more serious friendships, to everyday encounters with acquaintances, to romantic connections of all kinds.

But first, a little about me. I'll be honest—I've never been considered a very sociable or extroverted person, and identified as shy and a little awkward for most of my life. To me, it always looked like everyone else had received a rulebook for how to engage with others, and I'd simply missed out on getting a copy. None of it seemed natural or obvious to me, and I had trouble finding anyone or anything to spell it out clearly.

The book you're holding in your hands is the book I wish I had access to myself all those years ago. Back then, what I most wanted was a straightforward, no-nonsense explanation for how and why to socialize, the nitty-gritty details of communication, and concrete guidance on exactly what to do and what not to do.

Eventually, I decided on a "formula" format because this made the most sense to me. When you boil much of human engagement down to its essential components, you find that there are a few repeating themes.

The more I researched, the more I discovered that the world of communication and connection wasn't so vast and mysterious as I had previously thought. As I began to apply some of what I was learning, I discovered with some astonishment that it was working. I was more comfortable around others; I was making more friends and connecting more deeply with the ones I already had. I was finding myself feeling more understood and less often in conflict. I started to really understand what people meant when they threw around the term "active listening," and realized that, far from being the socially inept weirdo I always suspected I was, I could actually hold my own in any social situation—and enjoy it!

In the upcoming chapters, I'll share what I know about how to get things started, not just in a conversation but in a new friendship more generally; how to finetune your listening skills so that you're able to show genuine empathy toward those you interact with; how to tell compelling and entertaining stories, be funny, and even convince and persuade others round to your point of view; and how to gradually build up the strong, meaningful friendships that will matter most to you. I'll also explore some more tricky but inevitable parts of the process, including when and how to apologize, how to assert yourself when necessary, and how to exit a conversation or situation that's gone south.

That said, a few caveats before we continue. The material covered here is not meant to simply be interesting reading. It's meant to be *applied*. At the end of each chapter, there will be a summary encouraging you to revisit the main points but also to take concrete action, because I know that in the end, the real teacher is experience. Yes, it will be unfamiliar and a little scary at first. Yes, you may not get things one hundred percent right on the first try. I do encourage you, however, to adopt a curious, open mindset and be willing to experiment. Try things out, see what happens, adjust, then try again.

Be patient with yourself. While I know that these techniques, principles, and methods work (I know because they worked for me), I also understand that without consistent action, nothing ever really changes. The way we interact with others simply comes down to habit. Unless we actively do something to challenge this habit and practice doing something better, we will always default back to what we know.

So, on that note, I want to say that although a lot of the exercises and prompts may seem rather basic, their magic becomes evident when you take the plunge and bring them to life in your own unique situation. Merely reading a book about social skills cannot make you a more masterful socializer, right?

Challenge yourself, be patient, and most importantly of all, be consistent. Remind yourself that your obstacles, fears, and doubts *can* be overcome. Whether you're one of those people who claims to "hate small talk" and finds it excruciatingly difficult to meet new people, or whether you're the kind who meets loads of people but can never seem to retain them as friends, this book is for you. It's for you if you're looking to be more confident and assertive at work, but it's also for you if what you're really after is a cheat sheet for how to flirt, charm, and impress . . . or simply tell a good joke.

All that's needed is a curious, receptive attitude, some time and discipline, and perhaps a notebook to keep track of your insights and progress. If you're ready, let's dive in.

The Friendship Formula

Let's start at the beginning. Right at the beginning. Do you remember when you were a schoolkid? Cast your mind back to those days and recall the way you made friends back then. Think of your school friends and how it came to be that you considered one another friends in the first place. If your childhood was anything like mine, you probably have a tricky time answering this question. You were just friends with certain people because . . . well, they were *there*.

Maybe you went to school together and sat next to one another in math, or maybe they were a friend of your sibling, or a kid who lived on the same street. You probably saw them all the time without having to do much to be in their company. Perhaps you were even thrown together by pure chance, but you ended up bonding as a matter of course. Maybe you were both targets of the same bully, or you ended up stuck together on the long, boring bus trip to school every morning.

Fast forward to today. How do you make friends now, as an adult? I'm willing to bet that the process is not quite as straightforward. If you think about the people you currently have in your life, how did they get there and what keeps them in your orbit? Thinking now about those people who *didn't* stick around, why do you think that is, exactly?

Dr. Jack Schafer was interested in all these questions and more. He wanted to really understand what was going on when people "made friends"—with the understanding that if one knew, then one could deliberately engineer the best circumstances and, theoretically, make quality friendships more likely. Sounds like my kind of guy!

Schafer explored what he considered to be the basic ingredients required for people to hit it off and become friends. He condensed the findings of his research into what he called the Friendship Formula, and it's a great place for us to start our book. I've since discovered that it applies just as well to dating, too, with a few adjustments. The formula is pretty simple and goes like this:

Friendship = Proximity + Frequency + Duration + Intensity

Let's break down each of the elements in the formula:

Proximity: Proximity simply refers to the physical or social closeness between individuals. It involves being in the same place or sharing common contexts with someone. The more you are physically or socially near someone, the greater the opportunity for interaction and relationship development. Proximity can be established by simply being close to someone, even if you're not actively engaging in conversation. This gets a little complicated when you factor in online relationships; you can substitute digital proximity for real-world proximity to some extent . . . but, sorry to say, it's not one hundred percent the same thing.

Returning to our example, you can see why it's often easier for schoolkids to make friends with one another: They're always together. Five days a week, for hours at a time, they share the same places and spaces. For examples in adult life, think about working in the same office or even at the same desk, regularly bumping into your neighbor because they're always in the communal gardens you sit in, or connecting with a woman who attends the same reading group for babies at the library as you do, and at all the same times.

Frequency: Frequency involves the number of times you come into contact with a person over a given period. More frequent interactions provide more opportunities to get to know each other and build a connection. We'll see later in the book exactly why more frequent interactions can be preferable to less frequent, albeit longer, ones.

Kids in school see each other every weekday, for afterschool activities and sports, and even on the weekends, too. For another example, if you attend a weekly group fitness class, you'll see the same people every week. You might work on your laptop at the same café every morning and strike up a friendship with a waitress there just because you see each other almost every day. The regularity of these encounters can lead to friendships, as the repetition leads to familiarity.

Duration: Duration is all about the length of time spent together during each interaction. Longer periods of interaction naturally allow for more in-depth conversations and relationship-building. The duration of your interactions can vary from brief encounters to extended quality time. Schoolkids spend a huge chunk of the day together, as do people who work in the same place.

Intensity: Finally, this refers to the depth of the emotional or psychological connection created during those interactions. More intense interactions involve engaging in meaningful conversations, showing genuine interest, and fulfilling each other's psychological and emotional needs. But intensity can mean all sorts of things.

Have you ever noticed how people often don't really have much in common with their old school friends once they all graduate and move on? At the time, they served one another's needs very well—they mutually provided a sense of community and company—but once the school context dissolved, so, too, did their relationship. To return to our young mother at the reading group for babies at the library, she may form a very intense friendship with another woman in the same situation. This connection, however, may fade as their children grow up, and the women no longer have the same support needs as they once did.

Intensity and depth, then, are closely connected to the needs people meet for one another—needs that may grow stronger or weaker over time. Intensity can look different for all different kinds of people, from the deadly serious bonds formed in prison or in gangs, to a secret love affair, to a special friendship between college students trying to survive exam season, to the bond between a professional athlete and their full-time coach.

What's interesting about Schafer's formula is that it very clearly shows you that **each of these special ingredients can, to some extent, offset the other.** Colleagues at work may have very little in common and so have a low measure of intensity, but they make up for this lack with relatively higher levels of proximity and frequency. On the other hand, a long-distance couple may spend very little total time together in any given year, but when they are together, they spend long, uninterrupted blocks of time with one another (high duration score and high intensity score).

If you are trying to make friends, it's worth keeping Schafer's equation in mind. It's a reminder that often, the things we *think* are important when it comes to friendship really aren't. We may think that it's essential that our friends are very similar to us, or that we have to have closely matched worldviews, opinions, and preferences. We may think that it's up to us to be as charming and interesting as possible, and only then will we start making friends.

But this is misguided. If you've ever met someone you instantly "clicked" with, only to discover that it was really difficult to continue getting to know them, it's probably because something was missing—you were never in the same place enough times for a long enough time. It didn't matter how alike you were or how charming you came across. You could have the best single conversation of your life with someone, but without those additional elements, that initial connection would wither and go nowhere.

It may seem counterintuitive, but to use the insight in Schafer's formula means placing your efforts and attentions on things that genuinely will influence your ability to form friendships. Importantly, the ingredients are listed in the formula in their order of priority. Here it is again:

Friendship = Proximity + Frequency + Duration + Intensity

As a rule of thumb, you can start to grow a friendship first by increasing proximity, then increasing frequency, then the duration of each of those instances, and then finally, once everything else is firmly in place, increasing intensity. Though there are no hard and fast rules, mixing this order up can sometimes create awkwardness.

For example, there may be a new person in your distant social network that you're interested in getting to know. Let's say you meet them at some event or function one day, connect instantly, and then proceed to have a very intense conversation with them, where you blurt out all your secrets and share your most personal thoughts and feelings. This may work out okay . . . but chances are it freaks the other person out. The trouble is that you do not have enough proximity, frequency, or duration to warrant such intensity, and the other person is likely to perceive this soul-baring as a bit weird and intrusive.

In the same way, perhaps there's a new-ish friend in your weekly hobby group whom you're slowly getting to know better. Let's say you bump into them on average once a month and end up chatting for ten minutes or so each time.

Even though you have the proximity and the frequency, the duration and intensity are not there yet. If you were to invite this person to come along on an eight-day-long family vacation with you, the duration would be too quickly and drastically increased (from ten minutes at a time to *days* at a time) that it would feel like too much too soon. Expect awkwardness.

How to Use the Formula

Schafer's formula is a great rule of thumb. It helps you understand where you are with the people in your network, but also gives you a loose framework for the steps you might take on the road from stranger to friend:

1. First, just work on being around the person as much as possible, i.e., increase proximity.
2. Then, increase the frequency of these encounters.
3. Then, increase the length of these encounters.
4. Finally, change the quality of the encounters themselves by increasing their intensity, keeping in mind the various needs you and your new friend may be meeting for one another.

Here's how that may look in real life.

Imagine you've just started attending a local book club. You initially establish proximity by joining a group of people who share your love for reading. During these book club meetings, you work on increasing frequency by participating regularly in the club's gatherings and discussions. You build duration by staying engaged in conversations during these meetings, which can lead to longer and more meaningful discussions outside of the club. Finally, you deepen intensity by actively participating in book-related conversations, sharing your thoughts and experiences, and showing a genuine interest in the members' opinions. Over time, as you apply the Friendship Formula, you're likely to form strong friendships with some of your fellow book club members.

You may find yourself developing a friendship with one person in particular. You may agree one day to get a quick coffee together after a book club meeting, and by doing so you gently increase duration and frequency. You may, over the course of a few months, have a few more of these coffee meetups, and they get a little longer each time. You find, too, that you are talking more intimately and personally as you go along—the intensity is going up. Soon, at some point, you realize you consider this person a friend, and they think the same of you!

If you are currently trying to grow or start up new friendships, then look to the formula to help you understand what to focus on next. If you don't know anyone, focus on taking steps to simply be around others more; this is the old advice to join clubs, associations, and meetups. You don't have to do anything special—just be around.

If, however, you have some acquaintances already, you might use the formula to help you identify what part of the equation is strong, and which elements are yet to be developed. Could you try to gently lengthen the duration of interactions? Could you start proactively inviting people out more often? Could you increase intensity by opening up a little or sharing a bit more of yourself?

A few words of advice before we finish:

- Don't become a stalker! When I suggest taking action and "engineering" situations, I mean to invite people, to reach out, to create opportunities, and so on. If someone isn't interested or not currently able to connect with you, try a few times but don't push it.
- Be patient. Nothing is more off-putting than someone who is desperate to jump ahead to a sense of familiarity that isn't natural. Friendships take time. Try not to enter social

situations with a foregone conclusion of exactly where you want things to go.

- Pay attention. Often, less socially switched-on people can be blind to opportunities around them. Are there people in your world who have made efforts, no matter how small, to connect with you? It may not seem like a large anonymous hobby group counts as socializing, but it's a crucial first step. Practice saying yes to invitations and opportunities even if they don't seem particularly relevant. They may *become* relevant with time.

The Three-Part Formula for Small Talk

In the last section, I briefly touched on an idea that I think bears repeating: **When it comes to socializing, we have to start small.** Friendships are things that grow from tiny seeds. When I was in my early twenties, I found myself struggling to connect with others. I wanted big, juicy, meaningful conversations with people who really *got* me. I wanted a close bevy of best friends whom I could trust with my life, and what's more, I think I wanted this perfect social network ready-made, landing fully formed in my lap with zero effort on my part.

Growing up, I remember the ultra-strict mother of one of my closest friends, and how we'd laugh at her obviously impossible demand: "There will be *absolutely no dating* allowed . . . but also, I want you married as soon as possible." We could see the flaw in this reasoning: How could you ever get married if you didn't date first?

Well, I was busy in the process of making the very same error myself. I wanted to have deep and meaningful conversations with close friends . . . but I felt I was above "small talk." Socially speaking, I wanted to somehow marry without dating!

Look, I get it. Small talk can feel awkward and boring and superficial. In many ways, small talk can feel like an impediment to connecting with others. I assure you, however, that **small talk is what allows big talk**. This kind of interaction may seem trivial and unimportant, but I firmly believe it's one of the most underrated in effective communication. Small talk is not pointless. Small talk is not something annoying you have to do simply to be polite.

Instead, small talk should be embraced as an absolutely necessary first step in the long and sometimes complicated dance called communication. It's the step that breaks the ice, and its entire purpose is to be small. If small talk is small, it lowers risk and brings down that barrier to enter into conversation. It reduces the chances of a misunderstanding or even outright insult. It actually reduces the burden on you and allows both you and your conversation partner to subtly feel one another out, to gently ease into things, and if it doesn't work out, to bail without losing face or incurring too much loss.

Small talk seems like meaningless fluff, but it actually follows a very clear set of socially agreed-upon parameters. **The rule is that you pick a topic, provide some detail, and then quickly pass the turn to the other person, inviting them to contribute in the same way.** The purpose of small talk is to engage in a safe and predictable conversation with strangers or acquaintances, leading to deeper and more enjoyable discussions later. It's a social ritual that helps determine if two people are a good match for more profound conversations—think of it as a small conversation auditioning everyone for the larger conversation, or like tentatively building a bridge from one island to another.

Common small talk topics include the weather, origins (where someone is from), occupation or studies, hobbies and interests, popular media, sports, travel and holiday plans, current non-political events, current shared surroundings, and family-related questions. If you're like me, small talk makes you want to pull your hair out because it seems so . . . arbitrary. I used to resent feeling like I was suddenly on the spot and had to think of something to say to a stranger.

But you guessed it—I have another useful formula for you. These three steps will ensure that you never feel lost for something to say and can breeze quickly past that small talk phase—if you want to. The magic formula for small talk turns is to

1. **Answer the question**,
2. **provide one to two lines of additional detail**, and
3. **pass the turn.**

Those are three parts that you will find in every kind of small talk you might encounter. As the conversation progresses, turns can become more substantial, leading to more robust and meaningful discussions.

The person initiating the conversation (could be you, could be them) begins by asking a question related to a chosen topic. Once the topic is set, the key rules to keep the conversation flowing are providing detail and passing the turn. Providing detail is crucial because it gives your conversation partner something to work with and helps build a connection. Short one-word answers are conversation killers, while elaborating on your responses keeps the conversation alive and engaging.

Passing the turn just means asking a question in return. This back-and-forth exchange helps determine if the current topic is conducive to a more meaningful conversation or if it's time to switch to a different topic to find common ground. Ideally you want to keep things lively and quick-moving—don't hog the limelight too long!

One other topic I want to mention here is that **communication is never just verbal.** Try to observe two people engaging in small talk, and you will notice something interesting. The words themselves almost don't seem to matter. What does matter? The quality of the interaction itself. Imagine that you're watching the interaction on a TV where the language is switched to one you don't understand. Observe only facial expressions and body language. Listen to what the tone and quality of voice is saying.

People who are good at small talk understand that, yes, of course the weather is not the most thrilling topic in the world. But they are paying close attention to the openness of the other person's body language—their smile, the way they're leaning in, and so on. It's as though the superficial small talk is a screen concealing beneath it the real conversation, where we are all essentially asking one another, "Are you a friend? Are you and I going to get along?"

If someone engages you in small talk, remember that all you have to do is answer the question, provide one or two more details to expand on what's been said, and hand it right back to them. That's all. In reality, it often takes no longer than a few seconds. Be aware of your body language, too, and stay relaxed and open.

Them: "Oh my God, have you seen? They're saying it will snow tomorrow."
You: "I didn't see that! Uh-oh. Are they predicting a lot?"
Them: "I don't know. Says fifty percent, though."

Let's take a look at your response:

"I didn't see that! (Step 1—answer the question) **Uh-oh.** (Step 2—add some extra detail. In this case, just a single word!) **Are they predicting a lot?"** (Step 3—pass the turn back by asking a relevant question).

Now, I know this seconds-long exchange is not the greatest conversation you've ever seen in your life, but it does achieve a few things:

- You have actually broken the ice with this person and are now talking. A significant barrier has come down, and a certain momentum can now be built.

- You've shown that you're friendly and interested in them by responding warmly and appropriately.
- You've also shown that you'd like to carry on talking, and you're genuinely interested in what they have to say.

Paired with a smile and some open body language, the above exchange can be worth its weight in gold in terms of the connection it helps initiate. Let's see how it develops.

Them: "Oh my God, have you seen? They're saying it will snow tomorrow."
You: "I didn't see that! Uh-oh. Are they predicting a lot?"
Them: "I don't know. Says fifty percent, though."
You: "Fifty percent? I think that's the weather forecasters' way of saying they don't know! Do you have plans or . . .?"
Them: "No, no plans. Just wouldn't mind a day at home! Maybe they'll close the roads. Are you headed somewhere?"
You: "I am, actually. Going to [wherever] for the weekend, so I really hope you're wrong about this snow thing . . ."
Them: "Oh, you're going to [wherever]? I have an aunt down there. I think she's in [a suburb]. Do you know it?"
You: "Oh, sure, nice place . . ."

And so on. Gradually, almost imperceptibly, you are both slowly moving toward more meaningful topics. The beauty of small talk is that it allows you to arrive at that place gradually, and with no sudden movements! Of course, in this example, the other person was the one who went first. How can you be the one to get the small talk started?

Here's a solution for you, called the Office Small-Talk Generator. Following a straightforward chart, you can effortlessly craft politically neutral statements, share light-hearted and inoffensive jokes, and create spontaneous and memorable observations. While not all conversation-starters may be entirely logical, they are sure to add a touch of intrigue and fun to your day.

SMALL-TALK GENERATOR

PICK AN OPENING	PICK A QUESTION OR NON-SEQUITUR	PICK A BUZZY TOPIC
Hey! I'm so happy to see you...	Your haircut reminds me so much of...	Jennifer.
'hums a little ditty'	I've been meaning to ask how you're feeling about...	My pickleball team.
Stop me if I've already said this...	I'm just so happy things are looking up for...	Our competition.
So...	*silence*	That hot guy from Bridgerton.
Well, I guess I'll just come out and say it.	You know what I really missed last year?	My desk inmate.
Hmm...	Have you seen... ?	Oat milk.
I know this is kind of random, but...	These days, the thing I'm most grateful for is...	The weather.
[Deep sigh]	Do you want to see a hilarious TikTok about...	That email you accidentally "replied all" to.

Of course, the above table is just to give you an idea—you don't have to literally follow these prompts verbatim. What's more, you're obviously not going to be walking around with a little card to consult when you suspect that some small talk is about to happen! But what I like about the Office Small-Talk Generator is that it's a formula, which means you can plug anything into it and change it to suit any condition that arises.

You'll notice in this particular formula, they don't tell you to hand over your turn when you're done—this is taken as a given. Also notice that according to this formula, quite a few things can be considered "openers," including a deep sigh and simply saying "hmmm" or humming a little tune. Pushing this even further, an opener can, in some circumstances, be purely nonverbal and consist of a facial expression or gesture alone. Again, the idea is not to get hung up on the details, but to internalize the fact that successful small talk almost always follows this three-part structure.

Should you prepare small talk in advance? My answer to this is: yes and no. If you've met someone once before, and they mentioned something about their pet Pekinese named Chickpea, you might make a mental note to remember these facts—the breed of the dog, its name—and so the next time you spot them in a crowd, you can think to yourself, "Oh, there's the person with the dog with the weird name." You might then let this guide your small talk.

You: "Brrr . . . it's freezing in here. Did you know they're predicting snow tomorrow?"

Them: "Yeah, I saw the forecast. I hope it does. I love snow."

You: "Oh yeah? Do you still walk your dogs when it's snowy out? I remember you have a little Pekinese . . . Chickpea, right?

Them: "Haha, no way, she hates the cold! I have to put these little booties on her . . . I swear she gets embarrassed to be seen in them."

By doing this you can more or less continue any fledgling conversation you may have started in the past, but you also demonstrate loud and clear that you were paying attention, and this can be a powerful way to build trust and rapport. An extra side effect of recalling bits and pieces of information this way is that you lay the groundwork for potential "callback" jokes later. So, for example, a few weeks pass, and you bump into the same person. This time, your opener is something like, "Hey, nice to see you again. How is Chickpea? Have you found some more fashionable shoes for her yet?"

"Ha! Good one. She's fine, thanks. I keep telling her if she wants fancier shoes, she'd better get a job, but you know what dogs are like."

Now, this thread about a fashion-savvy Pekinese and her footwear adventures doesn't have to be rolling-in-the-aisles hilarious for it to strongly connect you and this person and create a feeling of familiarity and shared history. A lot of people misunderstand this about having a sense of humor—the bulk of the job is done simply by saying something slightly outlandish, unexpected, or incongruous to the situation (more on that later). You don't need to be clever, exactly; you just need to create a little shared moment between you and the other person, a little sparkle or secret that temporarily, in just a tiny way, creates a mini club that you are both a part of.

The Introduction Equation

Introducing Yourself

Don't you hate it when you're meeting someone new and you have no idea what to say? My personal idea of hell on earth was that thing that sometimes happens in meetings or groups, where the facilitator announces that they are going to "go around the table" and have everyone say a few words about themselves. I know I'm not the only one who sweats bullets waiting for my turn while desperately mentally rehearsing what to say when all those eyes finally turn to look at me.

I'll let you in on a secret—*nobody* finds this easy. In fact, if you've ever noticed that someone has an especially slick, confident-sounding self-introduction, I can almost guarantee that it's something they've deliberately practiced. First, let me clarify what I mean by an introduction. There are two kinds I'll cover here, the casual and the professional introduction. We'll start with the professional one, as this tends to create the most anxiety for people.

According to communication coach Andrea Wojnicki, there's a simple way to make this special kind of small talk easier for yourself. She advises breaking down your introduction into three parts: present, past, and future.

Your perfect personal introduction = Present + Past + Future

Let's take a closer look at what she means.

Present: This is where you start by mentioning your current professional status. In a professional setting, you typically state your job title and the company you work for. If necessary, provide a few relevant details about your role or responsibilities. Depending on the context, this may be something close to your "thirty-second pitch" or your "elevator pitch," i.e., that quick, simple summary of exactly what you do, why, and for whom. The idea is that you want to be able to swiftly tell a complete stranger what you're up to in a way they're likely to understand.

Past: Share a brief statement about your relevant past experience that adds credibility and helps establish rapport. This can be a concise summary of your professional background, or a slightly more personal narrative explaining your unique motives, your history, and any interesting information that gives context to explain why you landed where you did in the present.

Future: This is the part where you share something about your future interests or goals. It can be something you hope to achieve or a personal detail that you think will resonate with the audience. Again, depending on context this can help let others know what you're currently focused on or interested in and can give people a nice hook onto which to attach their introductions or follow-ups. This part should be kept short and sweet.

Remember that the key to a successful self-introduction is not just talking about yourself but focusing on what the audience in particular needs to know about you, and making it engaging and relevant to them. Naturally, you'll tailor what you say to match your audience and the context you're in. That said, you should always ensure that you've memorized a *general* structure for your answer and know what you'll say on the spur of the moment. Introducing yourself at an industry conference will be more formal and contain more specific terms than introducing yourself at a casual meetup with acquaintances . . . but the structure will be identical in both cases.

For example:

Present: "Good evening, ladies and gentlemen. I am John Smith, the senior project manager at ABC Corporation."
Past: "I bring over a decade of experience in managing complex projects, including our successful product launch last year."
Future: "Looking ahead, I am committed to driving excellence in project delivery and fostering innovation within our teams."

You can probably tell that this is the kind of introduction that would be made before a speech or presentation and may be tweaked somewhat for use in a job interview, meetings, networking events, or interactions with other professionals. When spoken out loud, the clear three-part structure is not evident to listeners, yet in a few moments, it gives them some context about exactly who you are.

If this same John Smith found himself casually striking up a conversation with someone at a parent-teacher meeting and discovered that this person may be a useful contact to get to know, he might change his introduction up a little:

"Hi. I'm John, Casey's dad in Miss Julie's class? I'm a senior project manager at ABC Corporation—I've been there for over ten years now, and we've just launched a new product not unlike the one I know you guys sell at XYZ Corporation. I'm always looking for new and interesting projects to bring to my team, so if you ever want to swap notes, it'd be great to meet up sometime."

This more casual variation may look completely different, but it's all the same elements as before, merely tweaked a little. Consider in this example that our fictitious John Smith is having to address this person in particular, and tailor his introduction to highlight the parts that would most be of interest to them, i.e., the connection between ABC and XYZ, and his willingness to possibly collaborate in some fashion.

In a way, formal introductions are much easier because the rules are clearer. You're required to include your full name and title, your job title, the organization you represent, a summary of your professional background, and your commitment to future goals or contributions— all the factual data that will help people place you. But you can also convey a lot about your motivations and personality in subtle word choices, and of course in your overall demeanor and body language. **Often, people who struggle**

introducing themselves do not need to phrase things better, but rather just say what they say with a little more ease and conviction.

You can use variations of your introduction in *any* context, so long as you're willing to mix things up a little. It's worth noting, too, that your introduction will likely change over time. It may sound cheesy, but it could be useful to keep a written record of your introduction. Spend a little time writing it out and then practice it a few times until it really rolls off the tongue. Then, think of various situations in which you might need it, and practice delivering this same core introduction but with minor changes. Don't forget to update as you go along. If there's some current achievement you want to showcase or a project that you're obsessed with, make sure it's reflected in your introduction.

Introducing Others

If you find introducing yourself especially tricky, you may never have considered learning the mirror skill—introducing others. While learning to do this correctly is a question of etiquette, it will also allow you to smooth over potentially awkward moments in conversation, and help you create good rapport and a comfortable atmosphere. If you're wondering whether there's a three-part formula for this, well, there is! Thankfully, introducing other people is a lot easier and less nerve-wracking than being in the spotlight yourself—if you can remember to do it, that is.

The formula:

Introduction for another person = Their name + An interesting fact about them + Something to connect them to the other person

So, for example:

"Kelly, this is John Smith. He ran this crazy marathon last year. I couldn't believe it. John, Kelly's also a runner, I believe."

Another example, although more formal this time:

"John, I'd like you to meet Kelly McDermot. She's our head designer for the new product launch. I suspect you both will be seeing a lot of each other in the coming months."

As you can see, the purpose of this kind of introduction is basically to do the other people in a social setting a favor—if done right, you are paving the way for them to pick up that conversation and run with it. Small talk between just two people can be daunting enough, but when there are groups with a mix of acquaintances, friends and complete strangers, the potential for misunderstanding and awkwardness goes through the roof. A good introduction like the one above not only makes things easier for the people introduced, but it also makes it easier for you, and others will notice and appreciate the gesture.

A few more tips for mastering introductions of all kinds:

Relax. I know this sounds obvious, but if you can smile and consciously open up your body language, it will reflect in your voice, and you'll feel calmer.

Keep it short and sweet. Introductions are not that different from everyday small talk. Your only goal is to give people a little context, convey a sense of friendliness, and move on swiftly. You don't have to tell people everything in just a few seconds!

Practice, practice, practice. The more you practice, the more you'll realize that a rehearsed response is actually an asset and a tool that can help you stay cool, calm, and collected in those tricky first few moments meeting someone new. If in any doubt, or if you fumble your introduction, don't worry—pass the turn to the other person and gather yourself. The hardest part is over.

Summary

- The things we think are important for forming friendships often aren't. Schafer's Friendship Formula goes like this: **Friendship = Proximity + Frequency + Duration + Intensity**.
- Proximity: Proximity simply refers to the physical or social closeness between individuals.
- Frequency: Frequency involves the number of times you come into contact with a person over a given period.
- Duration: Duration is all about the length of time spent together during each interaction.
- Intensity: Finally, this refers to the depth of the interactions and the emotional or psychological connection created during those interactions. Intensity and depth, then, are closely connected to the needs people meet for one another—needs that may grow stronger or weaker over time.
- Schafer's formula shows you that each of these special ingredients can offset the other. Try to understand where you are with the people in your network, and the next steps you might take on the road from stranger to friend. Place your efforts and attentions on things that genuinely will influence your ability to form friendships, focusing on the formula components in order. Be patient—it takes time.

- When it comes to socializing, we have to start small. Small talk is what allows big talk. It may seem trivial and unimportant, but it's essential for effective communication. If small talk is small, it lowers risk and brings down that barrier to enter into conversation.
- The small talk formula is **answer the question**, **provide one to two lines of additional detail**, **and pass the turn**.
- The perfect self-introduction follows this formula: **Your perfect personal introduction = Present + Past + Future**.
- The formula for introducing others is: **Introduction for another person = Their name + An interesting fact about them + Something to connect them to the other person**.

Chapter 2: How to be a Human Mirror (And Everyone Loves Mirrors)

The 43:57 Ratio in Conversations

When I was starting out on my social skills adventure, I devoured books that promised to teach me how to be a more captivating speaker, how to be witty and charming, and how to tell good jokes. I did my best to follow the advice in them, but somehow it never quite came together. It was only much later that I understood why: **The focus of these books was entirely on the wrong thing**. I had always been a little shy and unconfident, so I assumed that to be more sociable, I would need to learn to be more gregarious and outspoken and come across as more impressive and likeable to people around me. To put it bluntly, I thought that *if only I was more interesting*, I'd be more likeable, and socializing would be easier.

Big mistake! I began to behave as though every conversation was simply a platform for me to impress others. I had to make sure that they saw how unique, intelligent, confident, and funny I was. I had to let them know all my interesting opinions, and I had to shine as I told interesting, polished stories that made my life look really enviable.

Writing it all down like that probably makes it easy to see just why my approach didn't work! What I now know is that being a good conversationalist has very little to do with how interesting or impressive or sexy or intelligent you are. Instead, **a good conversationalist understands that their first duty is not to talk, but to listen.**

When I first started to practice active listening, I got it wrong. I'd sit there quietly, "letting" the other person talk, all the while I was thinking of all the awesome things I was going to blurt out the moment it was my turn. For me, I was still thinking that listening was simply not talking, and a small price you had to pay in order to earn the right to do what you really wanted to do, i.e., talk. The truth is that listening is as active and dynamic a process as talking—perhaps even more so.

Today I believe that genuine listening is in extremely short supply in the world. If you are able to really listen to people when they speak, you cannot help but create trust, good rapport, and a sense of liking with them. If you're in doubt about the power of listening, just ask yourself what *you* most want when you reach out to someone. Is it to learn about how great they are? Is it to sit and be lectured at length about the opinions they have on this and that? Or is it to truly connect with them, to feel seen and heard, and to have that wonderful sensation of being witnessed and understood by another person?

A good conversation is a co-creation. It's a give and take and a lively dance, where **the best attitude is one of playfulness, curiosity, and generosity**. I remember going to a party once and speaking with a woman I'd never met before. I decided I was going to treat her like the most important person in the world; I was going to listen as closely as I humanly could to everything she said, ask thoughtful questions, and do my very best to make sure she felt seen and heard. Truly, I barely spoke at all over the course of almost an hour-long conversation. The funny thing is this: As I said my goodbyes, she smiled broadly and said, "You know, I think you're one of the most interesting people I've ever met!"

Now, you can make of that anecdote what you will, but it's noteworthy that the thing I'd wanted all along was ironically only accessible to me the moment I stopped trying so hard to achieve it! Being unable and unwilling to listen often comes down to anxiety—we may worry that we are meant to always be speaking, always be saying something interesting or important, always broadcasting and defending our position. The secret is that none of this is necessary for an enjoyable conversation.

Try to remind yourself that a conversation is not a job interview, a slot on a talk show, a battle, or a competition. You're not trying to prove anything or teach anything or defend against anything. All you're trying to do is *connect*. That's it! The ironic thing is that when you allow yourself to just listen, you give yourself the chance to step out of the limelight, get off of any soapbox you might have been standing on, and relax into the interaction. Basically, listening is a clever way of dialing back your own anxiety, and this in turn will make you a better communicator.

In the world of sales, there is a commonly used guideline called the "43:57 rule," which recommends a talk-to-listen ratio of approximately forty-three percent talking and fifty-seven percent listening. This ratio suggests that successful communication, persuasion, and relationship-building can be achieved by dedicating *slightly* more time to listening to the other person's needs and viewpoints.

Good conversation = Forty-three percent talking + Fifty-seven percent listening (especially if *both* parties are striving for this ideal!)

In essence, the rule highlights the power of active listening and the idea that, in many situations, you are more likely to achieve your desired outcomes by giving the other person more room to speak and express themselves. Beyond that, you'll probably enjoy it more! While this ratio is not a strict rule (how would you keep track, anyway, right?), it is a valuable principle for better communication. Learn from my mistakes, however, and realize that the fifty-seven percent of the time you spend listening is not just time spent trying to spot a way back into the conversation again. If you're distracted by thinking, "Have they got too much airtime? Is it my turn to butt in?" then you're no longer focusing on what matters—the connection.

Here are tips to not only rebalance your talking-listening ratio in conversations, but become a better active listener.

Allow the Socially Awkward Pause

Allowing moments of silence (around three seconds) in a conversation can create space for a more meaningful discussion. Recognize that silence is where ideas incubate and conversations can develop. Just because someone has stopped talking doesn't mean they're finished communicating, and it doesn't mean that if they pause, it's fair game to sweep in and fill that space with your own ideas.

Give things space and time. Let the conversation breathe. A great idea is to consciously pause a few seconds after the point at which you think someone may be done speaking. This will allow a fuller pace to develop, but also signal to your conversation partner that you're paying attention, digesting the information they've just shared, and have priorities other than simply hearing yourself talk.

Another tip for the artful use of silence is to pause a little after you're asked a question. Pause a beat and just think of what you're about to say. If you comfortably take "the floor" in this way, you will also come across as far more confident and composed, because you will convey an ease with yourself. Interrupting or jumping in to speak prematurely, on the other hand, signals a certain anxiousness, doubt, and immaturity.

You don't have to become a solemn and plodding speaker. To the contrary, if you can mix moments of excitement and dynamism (talking more loudly and more quickly) with slower, more cautious speech, that dynamism and articulation will captivate your audience and help you really emphasize certain ideas more clearly.

Ask Questions Organically

Wanting to give the impression of being a good listener is not the same as being a good listener. Asking questions is good, but not just any old questions will do. The best kind of questions are those that actively demonstrate your listening and deep comprehension. Questions, then, are best thought of in the moment, and not scripted or rehearsed. If you ask generic and boring questions, your conversation will be generic and boring. If you ask a question because you sort of planned to ask it, then don't be surprised if your conversation takes a very predictable path. But if you ask questions that are dynamically connected to what you're being told, the conversation will grow and deepen and be far more successful.

Show genuine interest by asking for more details about what you're told. If you listen closely, you will hear the hidden emotional content of what the other person is saying. How do they feel? Why are they telling you what they're telling you? What does it all mean in their eyes? If you ask questions to expand your own understanding, then they will feel properly heard and understood. A great tip is to repeat the language and phrasing that they use in your own questions—literally, "speak their language."

For example, you may be listening to a childhood anecdote where someone uses the phrase "little troglodytes" with especial relish. You notice this turn of phrase and how animated they become when they use it; you find it interesting and unexpected. The question you ask is a direct follow-up, not just asking about this strange word choice, but also picking up on the emotion accompanying it and trying to connect it to the reason this person wants to gleefully tell you about how naughty they were as children. "Wow, what a fun word. It's like your mom was some kind of aristocrat from the eighteenth century! It sounds like you look back on those days fondly . . . Do you think you miss it?" This is a world of difference from a dry question such as, "So where did you grow up?"

Practice Empathy

Listening well is about centering the other person. Some of us are more than capable of listening and understanding what we're told, but we practice a kind of conversational narcissism when we simply switch the topic right back to ourselves after the person is done talking. You might tell them your mother was a literature professor and poet, and they'll listen carefully, but only to tell you immediately that *their* mother was a Red Cross nurse.

The habit of continually switching the focus back to yourself is one that can be difficult to put your finger on, but rest assured it will annoy, irritate, and bore your listeners. Even if people are only speaking half the time, they may do so in a way that starts to resemble conversational tug-of-war. There are broadly two kinds of conversational responses: a support response and a shift response. The support response keeps attention and focus on the other person and supports what they're sharing. A shift response is where you shift the attention and focus to yourself. For example, look at the two shift responses in a row here:

"I'm from a family of seven kids, so you could say things were a little chaotic!"
"Seven? Oh, wow. I was an only child, so it was really different."
"Well, I'm the firstborn, so I guess I was an only child for a while . . ."
"I really loved it, though. I never wanted a brother or sister."

Now, this is what the conversation would look like with two support responses:

"I'm from a family of seven kids, so you could say things were often a little chaotic!"
"Seven! Wow. And what number were you?"
"Number one! With such a great kid their first try, I don't know why they kept going, to be honest..."
"Haha. Maybe they kept trying to see if they could hit the jackpot again."

A shift response is not always a bad idea, but too many and you start to look self-absorbed and as though you're not listening. Mix it up. For every two or three support responses, add in a shift response—and keep your contribution meaningful rather than a complete derailment to your own pet topic. You could try making a response "sandwich" with a shift response tucked between two support responses. For example: "Seven? Oh, wow. I was an only child, so it was really different. What was it like for you, being in such a big family?"

Name the Feeling

People do talk to convey information, but the main point of conversation is almost always to meet some emotional need or convey some emotional information—even if that information is somewhat hidden at first. Naming and labeling this emotional content will let the other person know that you're paying attention to the deeper meaning, and that you care about what's being shared with you.

After you've asked them a meaningful, relevant question, verbally name the emotion you detect in their answer by saying something like:

"It seems like you _____"
"It looks like you _____"
"It sounds like you _____"

Even better if you can pose this as a question itself to invite them to confirm or add to your assessment: "It seems like being part of a big family was an ambivalent experience. Have I got that right?" or "Do you think that was a stressful time for you?" We'll go a little deeper into this technique in the next chapter.

The Basic Reflective Listening Formula

Because listening is such an important communication skill, in this chapter we're going to continue our discussion about exactly what we mean when we say that someone is a good listener. In the previous chapter, we covered the obvious bits: Listening means *not* interrupting, *not* making things about you, *not* talking too much, *not* asking boring or shallow questions, and not rushing to fill in every silence.

But what about all the things you should do?

Active listening is just that—active. It's something you do. In this chapter we'll consider the ways you can center your conversation partner, show them empathy, and really receive the message they're broadcasting, even as you're speaking.

Reflective listening is a specialized form of listening that involves paying respectful attention to the content and emotions conveyed in someone's communication. It entails hearing and understanding and then letting the other person know they are being listened to and understood. It's this second part that makes reflective listening such an active process, and different from what most of us would recognize as listening. Reflective listening requires active responses, focusing entirely on the speaker and refraining from offering one's perspective.

If someone asks you what the time is and you tell them, there's very little room for misunderstanding there—the data being passed back and forth is simple, and you are not required to look any deeper. Many conversations, however, take place at varying levels of depth well beneath this. People reach out and talk to you because they want support, validation, vindication, guidance, attention, soothing, advice, a reality check, or simply a kind and attentive audience to confirm that they're not alone.

Unless you can listen in and hear this unspoken emotional need, you will never connect as deeply as you could with those around you. Sometimes people talk to you about a situation or their perceptions on a situation because, in doing so, they clarify for themselves what they're thinking and feeling. In this way, your conversation with them becomes a kind of shared cognitive process—you are helping them think.

If someone has been doing an excellent job with active listening, they can say very little and merely reflect, and yet eventually the other person will wrap things up, saying, "Yes, I think you're right. I've decided that's what I'm going to do." You haven't told them to do anything, but by being able to witness, reflect, and engage dynamically, you have facilitated their own processing. In a way, this is the highest form of "advice" we can give people—to simply listen in a way that makes it easier for them to understand *themselves*.

To offer the other person this kind of deep receptivity and listening, we need to focus on three actions:

- We need to check that what we're receiving is what is actually being conveyed. That means hearing that person's truth without our own filters, perceptions, and assumptions laid over top.
- We need to confirm the person's emotional reaction to that truth—what it means to them and how they feel about it.
- We need to explicitly *connect* their emotional state to the content of what they're saying.

Now, all of this may seem pretty obvious, but in truth we can skip over one or all of these elements when we respond to people who are trying to communicate with us. It's time for another formula, and this one goes as follows:

Reflective response = Tentative check + Feeling + Connection

Take a look at the chart below for an idea of how you can capture all three components in a single concise sentence. For example, "If I understand you correctly, you're feeling angry right now because of what he said."

Basic Reflective Listening Formula		
Tentative Check	+Feeling	+About/Because/When + Thought
It sounds like	you feel mad	about
I hear you saying that	you feel sad	because of
If I hear you correctly	you feel glad	when
You seem to be saying	you feel afraid	about
I think I hear you saying	you feel confused	because of
I'm not sure I am follow	you feel ashamed	about
Am I hearing you say	you feel lonely	when

Now, I've shared this equation/format because, in the heart of the moment, it's a pretty foolproof default to fall back on. Empathy, however, naturally requires a little more of us than a stock response. Theresa Wiseman is a nursing scholar and what I'd consider an empathy expert, and she believes there are four main subtasks in the act of empathy:

Perspective Taking
This means being able to see and understand someone else's experience through their eyes, and not your own. This has sometimes been described as "getting in the pit." If someone is stuck in a pit, standing on the edge of the pit and looking down into it will merely help you understand that they're in there and probably don't like it. You might feel sympathy and have the thought, "If that were me, I'd be pretty upset," but you're not "in the pit" and seeing things from *their* perspective. It's the difference between seeing their situation through your own eyes versus seeing their situation through their eyes.

Nonjudgment

A big part of empathy is to accept and comprehend these perspectives, but without making a value judgment or rushing in to decide if something is right or wrong, good or bad. Sometimes we're in such a hurry to judge something that we are so much less able to just experience it for what it is. Judgments are about us and what we want and need. They usually just get in the way of seeing what's in front of us.

Emotional Literacy

Recognizing other people's emotions (as well as your own) and knowing how to communicate that. On a superficial level, this entails the kind of emotion labeling we discussed earlier, but it's more than that. Emotional literacy means being aware that in all things, there is a layer of meaning that goes beyond facts and logic, and concerns our direct experience, our needs and limits, our vulnerabilities and unique perceptions. Being aware of this layer is what allows you to communicate on a more three-dimensional level.

Empathy Is "Feeling With" Others

A psychiatrist may be the world's leading expert on paranoid schizophrenia, but when a patient tells them how terrified they are that they're being followed, the psychiatrist may have only a superficial, academic understanding of what this actually means.

Being empathetic doesn't mean we get lost in wallowing in other peoples' negative emotions, but it does mean we have to have a certain connection with our own emotionality and be able to draw on that when engaging with people. Feeling "with" someone is allowing something in yourself to connect with what is being shared with you.

Reflective listening is about being a mirror that we hold up to other people to help them better see what they're feeling and thinking. But we should not be detached and cold about it. With empathy, we're able to reflect in such a way as to communicate, "Hey, I'm here, and I'm listening. I care about you, and I care about what you're saying. You matter and what you're feeling is important. Tell me more." Without empathy, mere reflection can devolve into a disconnected, abstract exercise.

Validating statements are a way to show people that we see and hear them, and that their perspective, experience, and feelings *make sense*.

"Wow, I would feel the same."
"I can totally understand why you did that."
"That makes sense."

"Anyone in your position would feel the same way."
"Well, of course you're stressed. That's no surprise."

Sometimes the best thing we can say is not "I know how you feel" but rather to express that we cannot imagine how they feel, but we nevertheless hope to try and understand, and we're here anyway.

Now, I want to make a confession here. I genuinely used to believe that I was a kind person, and a good listener. But when I took a good look at how I was actually engaging with people and responding to their emotions, I had to admit that there was a lot to be desired! I felt very confident in my own position as a good guy and wouldn't hesitate to play armchair psychologist to anyone who dared to express a little emotional vulnerability to me. I now know that the most damage is not done by unkind or rude people, but by people who sincerely believe they are helping. Take a look at these responses and you'll understand what I mean:

A: "Some days I'm just not sure I can go on."
B: "Don't be silly, of course you can! I believe in you. You've got this."

A: "She had a miscarriage, and we're devastated."

B: "Well, God moves in mysterious ways. These things happen for a reason."

A: "This is the fifth time I've been ill this year . . . I'm miserable."
B: "Yes, but you have so many things to be grateful for. It could be worse, right?"

It took me a long time to recognize that these responses were designed to make *me* feel better—not the other person. I never realized that my "positive" responses were actually communicating something else to people: "Your distress is making me uncomfortable. I don't really want to deal with it or you." This was, in fact, profoundly invalidating since I was essentially judging people for how they felt, and telling them what I believed they should feel instead. Compare:

"Some days I'm just not sure I can go on."
"That makes sense, given what you've been through!"

"She had a miscarriage, and we're devastated."
"Wow. Thank you for sharing that with me. I can't begin to imagine what that's like, but I'm here if you'd like to talk."

"This is the fifth time I've been ill this year . . . I'm miserable."

"It seems like you're feeling really frustrated about being sick so often. I'm so sorry you're having to go through this."

These responses are different. They're not about fixing a problem, showcasing how awesome *we* are, or quickly brushing past the topic with some glib sentiment or cliché. These responses work because they're about connecting. They show empathy, and they validate the other person— not according to your perspective and perceptions, but according to theirs.

Be present, be focused. Imagine you're entering into that person's world. What is it really like to be them? To think and feel like they do?

John Powell has a beautiful quote that captures this idea perfectly:

> *"In true listening, we reach behind the words, we see through them to find the person who is being revealed. Listening is a search to find the treasure of the true person, as revealed verbally and non-verbally."*

The people in front of us may not be able to elegantly express exactly what they feel and what they need. But if you're attentive, non-judgmental, and totally present with them, you can "hear" everything you need to by attending to their non-verbal communication, too.

Here are a few more tips for empathetic, reflective listening:

Don't assume. Your frame of reference is different from theirs. XYZ means one thing to you, but a different thing to them. The only way you'll understand these nuances is if you bother to ask about them and listen to the answers. For a crude example, someone might say, "I've had a miscarriage," and get the response, "Phew, thank goodness! That was a close call!" This is strictly an empathetic response, but it's showing empathy for *your* worldview, not theirs. Don't assume anything. Instead, be curious.

Reflect non-verbally. You can "listen" with your body by mirroring the other person. Make eye contact, use open body language and mimic their expression. If they're talking low and slow, do the same. If they're frowning, reflect that, too, with a little frown of your own. Try to match their pitch, tone, volume, formality, and word choice. Sometimes this can communicate "I get it" more powerfully than any spoken words can.

Reflect both content and meaning. Remember that you want to connect these two and show that you understand not just the facts and details, and not just their emotional experience, but how these two things are related to one another. "So, you've had the flu *five* separate times in less than a year. It must be so frustrating for you to get better only to get ill again!"

Paraphrase and summarize. You don't need to add a single ounce of additional material to make someone feel heard. Repeat what they tell you in your own words, ask questions, (tentatively) label emotions, and finally, help them gather their thoughts by summarizing now and then. You can combine this with emotion-labeling. "It seems like this year has been especially challenging for you."

The Empathy Equation

We've seen that empathy is a special blend of perspective taking, nonjudgment, emotional literacy, and the ability to "feel with" others. It's from that place that we're able to turbo-charge our listening and reflect to others the responses that will genuinely make them feel seen and heard. In this chapter I want to take a closer look, however, at the different types of empathy—and when and how to use each of them.

Cognitive Empathy
Remember the psychiatrist who was an expert in paranoid schizophrenia? She would have what is often called cognitive empathy, where individuals make an effort to understand and *intellectually grasp* how another person feels. It involves putting oneself in someone else's shoes, considering their perspective, and

recognizing their thoughts, beliefs, and experiences. Cognitive empathy might not seem like much to some, but it's really the foundation of other types of empathy, as it helps individuals gain real insight into another person's world.

Often, what we lack is not exactly empathy, but rather imagination. We do not stop to consider that other people are simply not like us, do not necessarily share our values or priorities, and make meaning in a completely different way than we do.

Emotional Empathy
This is the type that people usually think of when they hear the word "empathy." Emotional empathy goes beyond cognitive understanding and involves a more direct experience of the emotions of another person. It means that you not only "know" how someone feels but also share in those feelings on an emotional level yourself.

As powerful as this form of empathy is, however, I want to make it clear that it is not superior to cognitive empathy, or somehow more real. Imagine what empathy would look like if it was only emotional, but lacked any intellectual grasp of the reality of a situation. Kind of difficult, isn't it? Emotional empathy without understanding may start to look like you mistaking your own emotional response for someone else's.

Compassionate Empathy

Compassionate empathy is the third type, where individuals take action based on their cognitive understanding *and* emotional connection. The secret to this type of empathy is that action element. It means using one's understanding and emotional resonance to support, help, or make a positive difference in the lives of others. Compassionate empathy translates empathy into tangible actions and behaviors, such as offering assistance, providing comfort, or showing kindness.

Plenty of people give advice or try to problem solve, but you can imagine that without emotional or cognitive empathy, you're not in the position to offer solutions that are genuinely in that person's best interest. Compassionate empathy requires that we care, but not so much that we lose objectivity or the ability to be of genuine help.

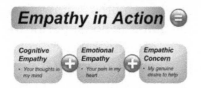

We can understand the empathy formula as follows:

Genuine empathy = Thought + Feeling + Action

The formula underscores the importance of *all three components* working together to create genuine empathy. Cognitive empathy provides the foundation for understanding, emotional empathy fosters a deeper connection, and compassionate empathy drives individuals to act upon their understanding and emotional connection in a caring and helpful manner.

Let's use the empathy formula to understand and apply empathy in a real-life scenario: A friend is going through a tough time because they failed an important exam.

In this example, the empathy formula is applied as follows:

Cognitive Empathy: Understanding your friend's perspective and the feelings associated with their exam failure. You might intellectually put all the pieces together and understand what they mean: The exam was important, your friend prepared for a long time, they feel insecure about this subject, and you know they were stressed on the day. You make a guess that they're probably feeling all sorts of things, from disappointment, irritation, and dejection to even stronger emotions like shame and despair. You also understand that, given that you yourself did well on the exam, it doesn't make sense to brag about this or to be insensitive when the topic comes up.

Emotional Empathy: Sharing in your friend's emotions and feeling sad or concerned for them. You might have passed, but they didn't. Can you remember what it was like to work really hard for something and still fail? Can you imagine what your friend is feeling right now?

Compassionate Empathy: Just because you feel bad for your friend, it doesn't mean it will help them for you to "get in the pit" with them and *stay there*, wallowing in the negativity with them. Instead, understand their position but realize that you also have the power to help them once you understand exactly where they're coming from.

What does that look like? Well, it will never be the same for any two people! If you have empathy, you can understand what an individual needs in a unique situation. Depending on what you know about your friend and their experience, the kindest thing to do could be reaching out to offer consolation, or it could mean keeping your distance and giving them space to process on their own. It could mean offering to help tutor them for the next exam, or it could mean lending them some of your study materials. It could mean none of these things, or something else entirely. If you have cognitive and emotional empathy in place, however, it means you're best positioned to understand exactly how best to make your friend feel seen, heard, and cared for.

Before we move on from this example, let's look at what happens when one or more elements is missing.

For example, let's say you only have cognitive empathy. Perhaps you're the teacher who gave out the grades in the first place. You understand perfectly well the upset that comes with a poor grade—you've seen it dozens of times—but you're not emotionally connected to it, and you're not taking action either way to help them. You say something factually correct, like, "Hey, don't worry about it. Most of the class did poorly on this one," but this doesn't really make the student feel any better or validate their experience in any way. It certainly doesn't change anything or give them a way out of their predicament.

What about if you only had emotional empathy, but no cognitive or compassionate empathy? Imagine that the student in this example has a baby brother who is not in school yet and cannot even read, let alone understand the complexities and challenges of a hard exam. When they come home upset, that little brother may be very concerned and feel that emotion strongly. The brother might offer plenty of sincere and well-meaning emotional empathy. But there is still something missing—the little brother doesn't truly *understand* the situation. And he certainly can't do anything about it!

Finally, what about compassionate empathy on its own? In truth, compassionate empathy is usually a result of the other two being in place, but occasionally it can be offered on its own, without any element of intellectual or emotional empathy accompanying it. Imagine our student consults a wise monk on a mountaintop who then tells him a Zen koan (parable or story) about a student and a master, one with a profound spiritual teaching hidden in its core. The student comes home and mulls it over and learns a lot about how to proactively move on from the challenges of failure in life. But this is not really complete empathy, is it? The monk on the mountain, being totally serene and detached, has little to offer in the way of intellectual or emotional connection, even though his help and advice may be extremely wise.

Summary

- Being a good conversationalist has very little to do with how interesting, impressive, sexy, or intelligent you are. Instead, a good conversationalist understands that their first duty is not to talk, but to listen. **Good conversation = Forty-three percent talking + Fifty-seven percent listening (approximately!)**

- Adopt an attitude of playfulness, curiosity, and generosity, and treat others like they're the most important people in the world.
- Give conversations time and space by allowing the occasional silence. Show genuine interest and ask questions that actively demonstrate your listening and deep comprehension. The goal of conversation is almost always to meet an emotional need, so listen for the hidden emotional content of what the other person is saying. Finally, avoid continually switching the focus back to yourself (i.e., shift responses) and offer more support responses.
- Active listening is just that—active. It's something you do. Reflective listening involves paying respectful attention to the content and emotions conveyed in someone's communication, whether their need is for validation, vindication, guidance, attention, soothing, advice, a reality check, or simply a kind and attentive audience to confirm that they're not alone. Simply listening can make it easier for others to understand themselves.
- **Reflective response = Tentative check + Feeling + Connection**

- There are four main subtasks in the act of empathy: perspective taking, nonjudgment, emotional literacy, and "feeling with" people, i.e., having empathy.
- Try to subtly communicate, "Hey, I'm here, and I'm listening. I care about you, and I care about what you're saying. You matter and what you're feeling is important. Tell me more." Don't make assumptions, and pay attention to your non-verbal communication, too. There are three types of empathy. **Genuine empathy = Thought + Feeling + Action.** Ideally, all three types are required, each building on the next.

Chapter 3: Connecting Underneath the Surface

The Secret Structure of Persuasive Communication

To recap, then, we've explored two very important principles for social success: understanding how to make friends (small talk, introductions, and increasing proximity, intensity, etc. over time) as well as your first main task once you make those friendships (i.e., listen and have genuine empathy). If you can fully master the concepts in the previous two chapters, you will have almost everything you'll ever need to develop and maintain sincere connections with others. In this chapter, we're finally ready, however, to consider some other skills and abilities that are a little less important but hold the power to drastically transform the way you engage with others.

Let's begin with the fundamentals: What's the point of connecting socially with another human being in the first place?

All of us have an inbuilt human need to connect with other people, whether that's family, friends, colleagues, or just acquaintances in our community. Some of us need a lot and some of us are happy with relatively less; our social needs may also change over the course of our lifespans. Nevertheless, it's something we all need for our sense of meaning, purpose, and well-being in life. What's more, when we communicate, we're primarily doing so to get our needs met—and these needs are often emotional in nature. **We reach out to others because we want to meet a whole range of emotional needs: validation, security, praise, support, companionship, recognition, respect, acceptance, privacy, intimacy, a sense of contribution and belonging . . .**

If all of this sounds pretty obvious to you, well, I have to admit that to me it wasn't all that obvious. You see, I used to think of social skills as, well, a *skill*—some kind of talent or ability that I could learn, like playing the piano or speaking Spanish.

While this is partly true, the trouble was my attitude toward other people in general. I sincerely thought that being a more socially capable person was something that had to do with *me* alone—a talent I'd acquire in my eternal *Project Self* quest for personal development. When it came to improving my communication skills, I mistakenly thought that the goal was simply to become very convincing and persuasive. I thought that I needed to come across as witty and intelligent, and "win" arguments, as well as make sure that I always held the right opinions and defended them perfectly in the company of those who didn't.

While this kind of thing may be appropriate when constructing a position in a formal philosophy exam, it took me a long time to realize that it actually had no place in the real-life world of human beings around me. I remember buying a book a few years ago that promised to improve the quality and internal logic of your communication and to present your case to others with clear, persuasive, and effective "arguments." It was a fascinating book, and I learned a lot from it. The big problem was the books confused "logical, persuasive argument" for "communication." Rigorously construct faultless premises and be able to withstand counterarguments and persuade your listeners to accept your position instead of theirs—this is what was considered successful communication.

I'm sure you can now understand why I failed socially for so long!

Let's return to our initial question—what is the purpose of connecting socially?

I'll concede that in a professional or business context, clarity of thought and logical consistency are extremely important. If you conceive of your communications merely as "arguments" in more personal contexts, however, you're not going to get very far. This is why I covered listening and empathy *first* in this book. Without them, it doesn't matter one tiny bit how "right" you think you are or how intelligently you lay out your premises. You will have failed to connect emotionally, and your communication will be degraded to an empty transmission of data—if that.

If you want to encourage others to think exactly the way you do, or your yardstick for measuring the effectiveness of an interaction is to check whether you got what you wanted out of it, then I recommend polishing your rhetoric and arguments . . . or perhaps going into marketing. If, on the other hand, your goal is to build friendships, connect socially with others, or even date more successfully, I recommend a different path.

The formula for "persuasive communication" that I learned goes like this:

Communication = Premises + Conclusion

The idea is that the foundation of persuasive communication is a sound argument that is able to change someone's mind. A premise is something that is offered as a proposition, hypothesis, or presumption about reality. Philosophers make sure their premises are sound and, if at all possible, true, and they look to attack their opponents' arguments by undermining the soundness of their premises.

A conclusion is the final statement that you want the other person to agree with, and flows logically from a series of premises, almost like a math equation. If an argument is persuasive, it will be because accepting the premises logically demands you accept the conclusion. There may be optional "inferences" included, which are extra elements of reasoning used to support the conclusion.

For example:

Car accidents do happen (premise 1).
A car accident may happen to you (premise 2).
If it does, it will cost you a lot of money (premise 3).

The cost of a car accident is usually less than the cost of car insurance (premise 4).

People want to spend less money instead of more money (premise 5).

By the way, we are having a car insurance special on for today only (extra inference).

Therefore, you should buy our car insurance (conclusion).

If you're a car insurance salesman (or someone considering buying care insurance), then this is all perfectly reasonable. You might take issue with premise 2 and say that it's not worth spending money to mitigate an outcome that only *might* happen, or you might quibble over premise 4, especially if the quote is really very high. Overall, however, the argument above is sound.

Here's the big question: Do you now buy the insurance? Have you been persuaded?

Let's consider another example:

Last time we went to the restaurant on ABC street, the food was awful (premise 1).

Last time we went to the restaurant on XYZ street, the food was pretty good (premise 2).

We want to choose the place with the best food (premise 3).

What's more, XYZ street is closer (extra inference).

Therefore, we should go the XYZ street restaurant for dinner tonight (conclusion).

Here's the question again: Do you think the above argument, being sound and logical, will effectively persuade your friend to go to the restaurant you want to go to, rather than the one they've got their heart set on?

A final example:

I gave red roses to a colleague (premise 1).
Red roses can sometimes represent victory (premise 2).
It is acceptable to want to congratulate a colleague on their work achievements (premise 3).
Therefore, I am perfectly within my rights to give the eighteen-year-old intern in a completely unrelated department at work five dozen red roses on Valentine's Day, despite my wife being devastated (conclusion).

Okay, that last one is rubbing it in a little, but I'm sure that by now, you're beginning to see where I'm going with this. Is it necessary to be persuasive, convincing, and logically robust in your communications with others? Absolutely. But it's not *sufficient.* By this I mean that there is a missing element from the formula we looked at earlier, because mere logic and reason are almost always never enough on their own.

The car salesman doesn't get your business because you can't quite afford his quote and, well, you just didn't like him much. Your friend might be unmoved by your explanation of why you need to go to XYZ restaurant because the reasons they wanted to go had nothing to do with the food or the proximity in the first place—it's the *ambience* they're interested in. And while you might be forced logically to agree with both premises in the third argument, any idiot can see that such sophistry might be superficially logical, but that doesn't stop it from being BS!

The missing element? Emotion.

If you're programming a computer or trying to impress a philosophy professor, pure logic and reason may be enough. But if you're trying to connect with a human being and grow a sense of trust, rapport, and harmony between you, then emotion is non-negotiable. Human beings are not machines. They're emotional, and they have emotional needs, and a lot of what they think, say, and do comes down to how they feel, and not exclusively the "facts of the situation."

That means if you want to connect with people, you'll have to acknowledge this role that emotion plays. Here's an updated formula:

Communication = (Premises + Conclusion) Emotion

In other words, your overall effectiveness as a communicator depends on your argument *multiplied by* the emotional connection you're making with the other person. Anything multiplied by zero is still zero. This formula, then, shows how even a strong argument can be reduced to nothing if the emotional element is not present. It also shows that if you've only got a weak or moderate argument, you can still be effective at communicating if you have a strong connection and are meeting people's emotional needs.

What does it look like to include emotion in your communication, though? It looks like understanding that

1. The facts and
2. People's emotional interpretation and experience of the facts

. . . are two different things. Nevertheless, the two are entwined. You will have noticed that the equation means that we cannot rely on emotion alone, either. Emotion without any reason quickly spirals into chaos and confusion, but reason without any emotion becomes dead and empty. You need both.

Communicating effectively has a lot to do with empathy. If you understand what the other person is feeling, how they're making meaning for themselves, and what the world looks like from their perspective, you are more able to talk *to* them. You will not convince them by more effectively outlining your own feelings, meanings, and perspectives. **Reason and emotion are not enemies; they feed off each other**. Our emotions tell us what we pay attention to and value, and the manner in which we interpret neutral data. Figure out how people feel, and you know something about how they think; understand how they think and feel, and you can begin to understand how to speak so that they can really hear you.

For example, the car salesman in the earlier example might notice that his prospective client is a busy mom of three kids. His empathy allows him to understand that she probably doesn't have money to burn, but that she might be receptive to "arguments" that center the thing that's most important to her: her children. If he connects with her emotionally and frames the benefits of insurance in terms of peace of mind and the safety of her loved ones, he's likely to be truly heard. If his prospective client is an arrogant twenty-something businessman, or a retired foreign couple with poor English, his arguments will take on very different forms.

In a more personal context, emotion is all the more obvious. If you're in a conflict with someone, chances are that both of you are feeling as though your emotional needs are not being met. You can resolve the issue by thinking carefully about what those needs are, and addressing them directly. Getting distracted by who is "right" and "wrong" or exactly what the facts are will only prolong a disagreement. This is because human beings tend to clash for emotional reasons first. Grapple with the superficial data of that situation without addressing the underlying unmet needs and you'll only go round in circles.

You might be wondering if there is an emotional component in professional or business contexts. Absolutely there is! The emotions may be different, however. Professional people are still human beings and make their decisions on the basis of what they *perceive* as trustworthy, authoritative, valuable, respectable, and so on— these are all emotional judgments. If you wish to come across as trustworthy to another professional, you need empathy and good listening skills to understand *what trustworthy means to them*. Until you do so, you will never really be persuasive.

Here are some practical tips, then, for using this formula in your own life and making sure that you're not forgetting to include the all-important emotion aspect.

- Whenever you talk to anyone, try to get a sense of the emotional need behind their communication. Why are they communicating at all? If you've practiced active listening and adopted an empathetic attitude, you may see that people seldom conceal these things, and merely paying attention will quickly reveal what people are wanting and needing from any interaction.
- As you talk, also try to make an educated guess about what they value and what their priorities are. This is essentially asking about their perspective and how their perceptions might be different from yours.
- If your goal is to cooperate with this person, to get them to like you, and to encourage harmony, then your goal should be to find a way to meet this need for them and to speak to their values, not your own—while simultaneously having your needs met and your values resected. In fact, if you continuously orient all your communication to this end, you will find it very hard to fall into conflict with people.
- If your goal is to defend yourself against this person, change their mind, or even manipulate them somewhat so you get your

way . . . well, you'll have to do all the same things. Understand where they're coming from and use that empathy to help you create an argument that will actually appeal to them.

- Liberally use terms and phrases that show that you're interested in harmony and collaboration, and avoid taking on an attitude of combativeness or defensiveness. Use the word "we" to show that you're on the same page.

- As a last resort, don't underestimate the power of simply being honest. Vulnerability doesn't make sense logically or on the battlefield, but it can do wonders at creating connection and diffusing tension. Sometimes the best way to get what you want is to just ask for it honestly and respectfully—no argument or explanation required.

I want to finish with an example to illustrate what this formula might look like in real life. Let's say you've just started a new job but for personal reasons need to take around two weeks off. You're not technically allowed to take leave this early in your contract, but it's a small company and you know that if you handle it well, you might be able to negotiate something. Now, you could sit down and think of a dozen logical and reasonable arguments for why you should have the two weeks off. Instead, you begin with what you know about the person you need to talk to: your boss.

You know he's a no-nonsense, proactive kind of person—you've been listening to everything he says, and you've been making conscious efforts to really empathize with him (and all your colleagues). Because you've paid attention and made the effort to genuinely connect, you know that your boss is a family man, but also that he doesn't appreciate weakness and excuse-making. You've seen him get annoyed with colleagues playing the victim or shifting blame. You've also noticed how much he loves dogs ("you know where you stand with animals!" he says) and that he seems most proud of his children when they show initiative and courage.

Taking all this into consideration, you construct your argument, *but tailor it to your boss*. Without beating around the bush, you come straight out and ask for two weeks' leave. You make sure you're not groveling or overly apologetic. You calmly go on to explain that there's been a death in the family, and you have some complicated obligations—but you are careful not to show any resentment or passive aggression about this. You present yourself in a straightforward way and without pleading. Without him asking, you suggest a comprehensive plan of how you will keep up with work as best as you can during the two weeks, and exactly what you're going to do on your return to catch up so that the disruption is minimal.

Your colleagues all think this is impossibly gutsy, but it works: Your boss hears you because he responds to the way you've made your argument. You are *speaking to his emotional need* for other people to stand on their own two feet, be honest, and so on. You are talking his language. It may be that on a personal level, you yourself would have preferred a far less direct appeal and would have apologized profusely and acted a little sheepish. But then you remember that this particular piece of communication is for his sake, not yours.

Your boss doesn't want to hear about how sorry you are or how bad you feel. He is more interested in how your actions are going to impact the office, and what you intend to do about it. He will feel vindicated by knowing that he has conscientious, can-do employees on his team, not people who are ready to spout off a dozen excuses for why they can't do their jobs. This simple perspective shift can be the make-or-break when it comes to persuasive communication. Someone else might have gone into his office with the exact same **premise + conclusion** part of the equation, but without the extra emotion, the whole thing might have gone far worse.

The XY Formula for Storytelling

This leads us nicely to our next chapter: the art of great storytelling. Here, I'm not just talking about commanding center stage as you regale someone with a ten-minute speech or cracking a good joke. Any time we are presenting *any* kind of narrative to our listeners, we're telling a story.

I'll be honest—I always kind of dreaded telling stories. I fumbled a lot whenever I sensed the limelight on me, and always seemed to mess up punchlines or get my details so mangled that the whole thing fell flat. These days, I understand a little more about why my stories so often flopped. First, I was anxious, and second, I was disorganized. Can you relate?

If you've ever found yourself rambling on and on as people's eyes glaze over and their attention drifts, I'd be willing to bet that you similarly suffer from both anxiety and disorganization. Sometimes, people believe that to be entertaining or interesting, we need to tell long and complicated stories. Nothing could be further from the truth—in storytelling, brevity really is the soul of wit! When I learned to relax, slow down, and keep things short and simple, my storytelling skills improved.

In this chapter I want to share a particular formula that I've found useful, both because of how simple it is and how it helps you keep your anxiety in check. The XY formula goes like this:

An interesting story = Subject + Captivating aspect about that subject

That's it, just those two elements, X (the subject) and Y (something interesting about the subject). I know what you're thinking: That doesn't sound like much of a *story*, right? Think of this as the bare bones of a good story—it's the juicy stuff that most people are really listening for. My stories, anecdotes, jokes, and narratives always fell flat because they were too long, took too long to get to the relevant part, and carried on too long after I'd already said the most interesting part. The irony is that I was working way too hard!

The XY formula comes to us from reporter and journalism instructor Alex Blumberg, who knows all about pitching stories to an editor. He calls this XY structure a "test"—if you can put your data into the format "here's a topic and here's why it's interesting," then you've got a story. Without the format, you've just got data.

On his website Blumberg explains,

> You simply tell someone about the story you're doing, adhering to a very strict

formula: "I'm doing a story about X. And what's interesting about it is Y."

So for example . . . "I'm doing a story about a homeless guy who lived on the streets for ten years, and what's interesting is he didn't get off the streets until he got into a treatment program." Wrong track. Solve for a different Y.

Y = ". . . and what's interesting is there's a small part of him that misses being homeless." Right track.

Y = ". . . and what's interesting is he developed surprising and heretofore unheard of policy recommendations on the problem of homelessness from his personal experience on the streets." Right track.

Y = ". . . and what's interesting is he fell in love while homeless and is haunted by that love still." Right track.

Y = ". . . and what's interesting is he learned valuable and surprising life lessons while homeless, lessons he applies regularly in his current job as an account manager for Oppenheimer mutual funds." Right track.

Of course, Blumberg is a journalist, and his business is to create newsworthy articles. But he can teach us a lot about what makes a good story work . . . and why a bad story is bad. Unless there is something genuinely new, interesting, captivating, unexpected, or emotionally relevant in a narrative we're sharing with someone, it's not going to hold their attention for very long.

Once you start thinking of things in terms of this XY structure, you'll realize a few common mistakes when people tell stories, whether that story is a joke, an anecdote, a moving tale, an explanation for something, or an attempt to convince or entertain:

1. Just because someone is talking doesn't mean there is a story there. Just because one thing happens and then another thing happens doesn't make it a story!
2. A character, a place, or an incident on its own is not automatically a story—that's just the X part. You can't assume that the Y is given, or that people can fill in the blanks and guess what it is.
3. Don't tell the boring parts first.
4. Remember that not every story needs to be told.
5. Lastly, even if a story does follow the XY format, it doesn't guarantee that it will be an *excellent* story, just that it will be a story (more on this later).

The magic of the XY Story Formula is that it's concise and pushes you to distill the essence of a story down to (usually) two sentences. In the first sentence, you identify the subject or topic (X) of your story, which can be anything from a person, event, or general subject area. In the second sentence, you highlight what makes the story compelling (Y) by pinpointing an element that is surprising, unexpected, or otherwise captivating.

Both parts are vital here, and it's important they're in this order. Introducing the topic first seems like a no-brainer, but too many of us speak as though we're writing a novel, where we should speak as though we're delivering a journalist's bulletin: All the important contextual information should be given first.

The second part is also extremely important because it essentially tells your listener why they should care. What's the point of the story, and why are you telling it? A good mini story of this kind is one where it's easy to tell that it's over. The people who end up droning on and on? They're missing that crucial Y component in the formula. Their listeners are no longer paying attention because they have started to doubt that there is anything surprising, unexpected, or otherwise captivating on the horizon!

The XY Story Formula is great because it encourages you to find that unique and intriguing angle within a topic or event, ensuring that your narrative is as captivating as it can be. It's a discipline that also forces you to "cut to the chase" and be very clear about the gist of what you're sharing.

You can incorporate the XY Story Formula into normal conversations to make your storytelling that little bit more engaging and concise. It can help you quickly convey the essence of a topic or story to your audience. Here's how you might use it in a casual conversation:

Friend: "So, what have you been working on lately?"
You: "I've been working on a project about renewable energy (X), and what's interesting about it is that a small town in Texas powered entirely by wind turbines has become a model for sustainable living (Y)."

In this conversation, you've introduced your project, provided the subject (renewable energy), and highlighted what makes it intriguing (the sustainable town acting as a model). This format not only helps your friend understand the core of your project in a concise and engaging way, but it also provides enough narrative structure to keep him interested.

Without the XY structure, you could risk saying something like:

"Well, you see, there's this town that is using renewable energy to supply all its energy needs—that includes *everything*, powering the whole town—and it's in Texas, right? It's called Georgetown. I wonder if you've heard of it. They did a story recently in the paper; maybe you saw it? Anyway, because I'm doing an environmentalism degree, they've asked us to research interesting real-life case studies, and I chose Georgetown. They wanted us to find some examples and show what they had done right and that kind of thing. You know how it goes . . . The article in the paper wasn't a fair reflection, by the way, but anyway . . ."

If you were to listen to the above "story," what would you think? A few things:

- It's unclear what the point really is—where's the focus of the story? Are you wanting to draw attention to your degree, to the newspaper story, to Georgetown? It's not at all obvious. Problem: it's unclear what X, the topic, is.
- It's also unclear *why* you're sharing this story. What's the punchline, so to speak? Problem: it's unclear what Y, the interest, is. The listener is going to be struggling to see why they should continue to pay attention. When does this story end?

Another possible outcome is that you blunder and say something like, "Uh, er, I'm working on renewable energy," which leaves your listener with the task of trying to figure out what makes that interesting . . . and that's your job! Without a clear X, a clear Y, and a clear connection between the two, you risk coming across as boring, or else like someone who's only interested in hearing themselves talk. In fact, the next time you're in a conversation with someone and you're feeling it becoming tedious, quickly ask yourself if you can identify the X and the Y of each contribution they make to the conversation—chances are you'll spot the problem immediately.

Now, I want to share something that I'm a little bit embarrassed about, but perhaps you can identify with me. I'm the kind of person who tends to keep to myself, and I don't dominate conversations at all, but if someone asks my opinion on something I'm passionate about or have a lot of experience with, then I find myself going into what I'll euphemistically call Lecture Mode. Perhaps you can already predict what I mean by this . . .

I consume a fair number of podcasts and YouTube videos, I read and listen to audiobooks, and I like watching talk shows and interviews. Though I learn a lot this way, I've also realized that this has given me a skewed expectation of what natural human conversation should and could be like. When I notice that the topic has switched to something I know a lot about, my brain suddenly kicks into gear and says, "Hey, you're an expert in this!" and it suddenly starts generating tons of ideas, facts, and opinions related to the topic. The result is predictable: I talk a little too long and a little too intensely on topics that I haven't bothered to check are interesting to anyone else. I'm no longer telling a story—I'm just lecturing. Sound familiar?

The truth is, we are all living in an information-saturated world. There's a lot of data out there, and we are all blessed with limited time, attention, and processing power. What this means is that **receiving a person's attention is actually a privilege**. It may be harsh, but why should they listen? Most polite people will humor those in their social circle for a little while just to maintain harmony, but you can hold yourself to a higher standard. Continually ask yourself, what's surprising? What's different here? If you think like a journalist, you'll see that there are in fact no new topics under the sun . . . but the angle on these topics can always change. A good story relies on you identifying that and presenting it to your listeners in such a way that they'll be captivated and glad they invested their time and attention into hearing it!

. . . But Interesting to Whom?

Let's look at this example again:

"I've been working on a project about renewable energy (X), and what's interesting about it is that a small town in Texas powered entirely by wind turbines has become a model for sustainable living (Y)."

Now, do you find it *interesting*? Well, that depends on who you are! If you're an investor in wind energy, a person who lives elsewhere in Texas, or someone who's also doing an environmentalist degree, then you may well find this interesting. But not everyone will.

The secret to a good story is to highlight what's interesting, but human beings decide what is interesting based on one thing: emotions. A thing becomes interesting *because* a listener is engaged with it emotionally. You may as well understand "interesting" to be code for "engages this particular person emotionally." In other words, there is nothing universally interesting. To be good storytellers, we must understand who our audience is, what matters to them, what they feel about certain situations and topics, and how they are likely to respond to hearing your story. And here we are again, back to the fundamental skills of listening and empathy!

When people pay attention to something, on some level they are all thinking, "What's in this for me?"

If you can understand that, then you can tell a good story. So, if you know that the person in front of you doesn't care at all about environmentalism and isn't really emotionally connected to wind energy or what people are doing in Texas, then you may either a) tell them a different story or b) tell them this story but angle it so that they care.

"In Georgetown, there's this old church on Q Street called the *Church of Two Worlds*, and it still practices what's called Spiritualism. What's interesting about that is it basically means you can attend a real-life séance there."

For the right kind of person, the above ministory is very interesting, indeed!

The LOL Formula

If we're talking about communication, emotion, and connection, then we have to talk about humor. Laughter is a human social behavior that seems simple on the surface but is actually rather complicated. **Laughing serves many different functions** and is not merely a response to something amusing. People laugh in response to embarrassment, out of politeness, when they're nervous, and to indicate derision or mockery. Amused laughter often arises not because something is genuinely funny but as a response to a "benign violation," signaling that a situation, though potentially threatening, is safe. It's a way to ease tension, maintain harmony, and defuse minor mishaps that could become more serious.

When we laugh, it's a kind of "play signal" that communicates that things aren't so serious, that there is no threat, and that everyone is comfortable and enjoying themselves. Laughter, then, is a kind of **social lubricant**.

In fact, this term "humor" has a more nuanced history and was used in the past to indicate a person's overall mood, disposition, and state of mind. The bodily humors were understood to be the physiological elements making up a human body—if you were healthy and well, you were said to be in good humor. More broadly, then, humor can be understood as a kind of attitude, a force of ease and well-being, a flow, and a frictionless and pleasant state of being. I begin with this more *social* and even *psychological* definition of humor because I want to emphasize the ideal attitude to bring to any attempt to be funny. Understanding what humor is for and how it functions will help you become better at creating it.

Have you ever engaged socially with someone who was desperately playing "the clown," except their attention-grabbing antics only annoyed everyone? Unskillful or misguided attempts at humor can be disastrous. It's not that the person isn't "funny," however; it's that their approach is all wrong. By centering themselves and putting their own ego first, they are inverting the true function of humor—to be a social lubricant—and instead creating friction. Good humor is something you contribute to the conversation; poor humor is an attempt to extract something from the conversation.

Changing the way you think about humor in social situations actually means you can take a lot of pressure off yourself. Being a good conversationalist does not require that you're entertaining, funny, or witty. You don't have to be exciting or a loudmouth or over-the-top or super popular. You definitely don't need to tell jokes!

But what you do need to become skillful at is learning to cultivate an atmosphere and mood of good humor. You need to know how to lubricate social situations, more or less!

As it happens, this is not about putting *you* in the limelight so that you can entertain people, but rather it entails making *other people* feel at ease by bringing levity and playfulness to the moment and allowing a certain spontaneity and relaxation to guide your conversation, instead of ego or anxiety. So, the most important thing about humor is that it's first and foremost a mindset. It's basically impossible to be humorous while also taking yourself too seriously, having a big ego, or being choked with anxiety because you feel you need to perform.

The next thing you can do to become a funnier person is to follow the humor formula, or as I like to call it for no reason in particular, the LOL formula. It shows the relationship between the normal, the absurd, and specificity. Let me explain. In comedy, the "normal" is the everyday situation or behavior, the "absurd" is the exaggerated deviation from the normal, and "specificity" adds a unique and detailed touch to the absurdity.

Funny = (Normal + Absurd) Specificity

Let's break it down with examples:

The Normal: This is the starting point, where you establish a relatable or common scenario.

The Absurd: Comedy kicks in when you take the normal and exaggerate it to an extreme level.

Specificity: This is the key ingredient that makes the humor work. It involves adding unique, unexpected, and detailed elements to the absurd situation.

Let's look at an example—a comedy skit by Key and Peele (titled "I Said Bitch").

The *normal* is established first: Two couples meet one day, and the women group up and wander off, leaving the men to subtly gripe about them out of earshot. Both men exaggerate how bad their partners are, but also exaggerate how they pushed back: "I looked her in the eye, and I said, bitch . . ." to impress the other. "Woah, but did you *really* say bitch to her?" The mild humor here is that they lower their voices, look over their shoulders, and mutter this word quietly, clearly indicating that they have said no such thing and never would dare. So far so good—pretty normal.

The *absurd* enters in stages, where the same scene above is repeated, only each time it gets more and more outlandish. The men are increasingly far away from their partners—in a cellar, up a tree, eventually in outer space—and yet they're still terrified of their partners overhearing them. The conversation is essentially the same, but the details are getting more ridiculous. First, he "looked her in the eye," but in subsequent conversations he looks her in the "eye socket," then he looks her in the "optic nerve," and finally "I looked this woman dead in the windows of her soul."

There's more *specificity*, too, in the anecdotes the men are telling—the tired old arguments about a woman taking too long to get ready are made all the more real and engaging by giving the specific details of the time he had to wait, the restaurants they went to, and so on. It's a funny skit, it's totally ridiculous, and it relies purely on the LOL formula, nothing more.

To ensure your humor works effectively, you can use this formula as your compass. A great thing to realize is that you can inject humor and silliness into things without necessarily having a punchline pre-prepared. The equation tells you that funniness is a balancing act. If your comedy feels too ordinary, infuse it with more absurdity. If it's too bizarre and without grounding, add specificity to connect it with reality. You can apply the LOL formula in a casual conversation to add a touch of humor to everyday interactions. Here's an example:

Normal: Talking about a typical morning routine.

Absurd: Exaggerate an aspect of the routine to an extreme level. Let's say you're talking about your friend's habit of hitting the snooze button multiple times before getting out of bed. You could exaggerate this by saying, "You won't believe it, but every morning, it's like a snooze button battle royale at my place. My friend sets so many alarms that it sounds like a fire drill in a chicken coop."

Specificity: The humor here comes from the specific details: comparing the alarm noise to a fire drill in a chicken coop. These specific comparisons add a unique and unexpected twist to the exaggerated situation.

One variation on the LOL formula is to lean into *subversion* rather than *absurdity*.

To do this, all you need is to identify what the normal is and then completely turn that on its head. While this is the realm of sarcasm (saying the opposite of what you actually mean), subverting expectation is a lot more than that.

First you set up an expectation (the normal), and then you surprise your audience with something completely at odds with that. Alternatively, you can respond to something in a way that is completely out of the ordinary. If someone walks into the office and sees the cast on your foot and asks, "Oh no, did you break your foot?" you can act all nonchalant and say something like, "No, I just love the way the bandages bring out the color in my eyes. Foot casts are all the rage on the catwalk in Milan this year, don't you know." It's funny simply because nobody will be expecting this response.

There's a cute quote from Robert Benchley that goes "a boy can learn a lot from a dog: obedience, loyalty, and the importance of turning around three times before lying down." What makes this funny? Human beings have a natural understanding for the narrative power of the number three. Benchley uses this expectation to get his audience to listen for the third virtue that might fit alongside loyalty and obedience. These expectations are subverted in the final item on the list, and this creates a tiny moment of pleasant shock—it's where the humor is.

More examples of subverted expectations:

"When I was a kid, my parents always moved around a lot. I always found them again, though."

"This bully at work keeps calling me gay, and I've had enough. I'd punch him in the nose if he wasn't kinda cute."

"I haven't spoken to my wife in years. I didn't want to interrupt her."

Can you see the setup immediately followed by the subversion?

Laughter as a Kind of Communication
Before we move on, let's consider one final point that's worth understanding—the power of laughter as a communication device. When you laugh at something or someone, you also have the opportunity to send useful signals and shape your social interactions. According to theorist Adrienne Wood in a 2018 research paper (*Social and Personality Psychology Compass*), there are three main social functions of your laughter:

> "We propose that the first social function of laughter, both evolutionarily and developmentally, is to *reward* the behavior of others and reinforce the ongoing interaction. The second task accomplished by laughter is the easing of social tension and signaling of *affiliation* and nonthreat. A third form of laughter nonconfrontationally enforces social norms, negotiates status, and corrects undesirable behavior in

others by conveying *dominance* or superiority."

Reward laughter is about cultivating a feeling of pleasure. Laughing at other people's jokes or stories sends a clear message that you're comfortable with them, like them, and consider them safe.

Example: Your date is telling you a silly anecdote about their childhood, and you listen closely, laughing often.

Try: Laugh whenever you want to send the message "I'm enjoying your company" or "I acknowledge and appreciate you."

Affiliation laughter sends roughly the same message, but it's less about good feelings and more about reassuring, soothing, and appeasing people. To be affiliated means to belong to the same social group; this kind of laughter recognizes that.

Example: The bus breaks down, and you chat a little with the other passengers, throwing your hands up and laughing to lighten the mood.

Try: Laugh whenever you want to send the message "I'm with you on this" or "I understand you exactly."

Dominance laughter is a trickier one, and something you hope not to use if you can help it. Laughing at someone is a way to undermine or hurt them, and should be avoided. It's not great to use laughter as a weapon, but very occasionally it might be the only way to offer a critique while maintaining a certain level of etiquette.

Example: The airport official is explaining how they accidentally lost your luggage. You laugh derisively.

Try: Laugh this way when you want to send the message "this is ridiculous" or even "you're ridiculous."

By the way, there is no such thing as a "fake laugh." While some kinds of laughter are extremely uncontrollable, all laughter forms serve their purpose and are as real as any other form of communication.

Summary

- Social connection is something we all need for our sense of meaning, purpose, and well-being in life. The goal of any social interaction is to meet these needs, not to convince, persuade, win, or impress others. It's not enough to construct faultless premises, withstand counterarguments, and persuade your listeners to accept your position instead of theirs. Being logically robust in your communications with others is necessary but not sufficient—you have to include emotion, too.

- **Persuasive Communication = (Premises + Conclusion) Emotion.** Your overall effectiveness as a communicator depends on your argument *multiplied by* the emotional connection you're making with the other person. Understand the "facts" but also people's experience of the facts.

- Communicating effectively requires empathy. If you understand what the other person is feeling, how they make meaning, and their worldview, you are more able to talk *to* them so they will hear you. Tailor your arguments to appeal to people's emotional needs and values directly.

- Any time we are presenting *any* kind of narrative to our listeners, we're telling a story. For good stories, relax, slow down, and keep things simple. **An interesting story = Subject + Captivating aspect about that subject.** Put your story into the format "Here's a topic and here's why it's interesting."

- Unless there is something genuinely new, interesting, captivating, unexpected, or emotionally relevant in a narrative we're sharing with someone, it's not going to hold their attention for very long. Be concise and find your unique angle. Keep in mind that what's "interesting" depends on your listener.

- Laughter serves many functions but is a primal "play signal" that communicates that things aren't so serious, there is no threat, and everyone is enjoying themselves. Laughter is a social lubricant. Humor is a mindset incompatible with taking yourself too seriously, a big ego, or anxiety. **Funny = (Normal + Absurd) Specificity.**

Chapter 4: On Helpful Balances for Pleasing Interactions

The Magic Relationship Ratio

Psychologist and professor Dr. John Gottman is widely considered a relationship guru and has probably saved more marriages than he can count. His advice, however, is applicable to any type of relationship. His "5:1 rule" suggests that for a relationship to remain stable and healthy, there should be a minimum of five positive interactions for every one negative interaction. Of course, this is not to say you should aim to have a certain number of negative interactions; instead this ratio explains just how damaging a negative interaction can be to overall harmony and connection, and just what it takes to neutralize its effects.

Negative interactions that can harm relationships include being emotionally dismissive, stonewalling, expressing contempt or defensiveness, exaggerated complaining, negative body language, and using "yes, but" remarks. On the other hand, positive interactions that foster healthy relationships involve asking about each other's day and genuinely listening, showing affection and kind gestures, offering intentional words of appreciation, apologizing when necessary, and sharing laughter and playful teasing.

While this ratio isn't an absolute law, it's a helpful guideline for maintaining positive and nurturing connections with others. It reminds us that a relationship—any relationship—is a living, breathing thing that needs to be cared for and maintained over time. If any relationship is continually subject to too many negative interactions without much positive to counterbalance it, the only possible outcome is for it to fizzle and burn out.

Gottman's formula is not so much an equation as a ratio:

A healthy relationship follows the ratio of 5:1, with AT LEAST five positive interactions for every negative one.

Let's take a closer look at what exactly Gottman was trying to explain with this ratio. Where negative interactions are concerned, he identifies four types, which he calls the Four Horsemen. These behaviors are signs of trouble in a relationship and can lead to conflict and dissatisfaction.

The Four Horsemen are:

- Criticism
- Defensiveness
- Contempt
- Stonewalling (ignoring or "silent treatment")

According to Gottman, the presence of these behaviors in a marriage strongly predicts divorce, but there's no reason to think that a friendship or family relation won't follow the same principles. While occasional negative interactions are normal in any relationship, **a *persistent* presence of these behaviors can be detrimental to the relationship, especially if they are never offset by anything positive**.

To counteract the negative effects of a single negative interaction during conflict, you need to consciously follow it up with five positive interactions. Positive interactions help to de-escalate tension and restore a sense of connection. Dr. Gottman recommends the use of "repairs" during conflicts, which are statements or actions that de-escalate the tension and get the discussion back on track. Some examples of positive interactions and repairs include:

- Gestures of appreciation
- Showing affection
- Checking in with the other person (and really listening!)
- Being present and engaged
- Doing something thoughtful for one another
- Focusing on the positives

Perhaps you've noticed something interesting here. All relationships will eventually experience some kind of conflict or misunderstanding. What matters, however, is how each party responds to this and what happens next.

Example 1: Two friends get on extremely well, but occasionally they have an argument, let's say around once a month. In that same month, there are also happy and positive interactions, about one every week. Their ratio of positive: interactions to negative ones is around **4:1.**

Example 2: A second pair of friends also gets on well, but they have more frequent arguments, let's say once every week or so. However, in a month they tend to have a happy and positive interaction almost every day. Their ratio of positive interactions to negative ones is 30:4, or to simplify, almost **8:1**.

The pair in the second example argue far more, but their ratio is much healthier than the first example. The first pair of friends may actually end up drifting apart over time (since their ratio falls below Gottman's crucial 5:1 ideal) even though the absolute level of conflict is pretty low. Though this is obviously an oversimplification, you get the idea: It's not the number of interactions that matters, but their relative proportion.

Naturally, an even better outcome is a third example, where two friends have a disagreement or misunderstanding once every year or two, yet rack up positive interactions at a rate of two dozen a month. Their ratio will be closer to **300:1**. That single disagreement, in other words, doesn't have a chance of causing much trouble!

What can we do with this information? There are a few insights to be gleaned from Gottman's expertise, and they apply just as well to casual acquaintances as life partners and family members:

Negative interactions are normal and natural. Even in the best friendships or relationships, some friction will occur now and again. This in itself is not a problem.

It's your responsibility to monitor and manage these negative interactions. Though they're inevitable, we cannot be passive and let these regrettable moments accumulate like bad debt. Another analogy is to think of it like housework—unless you regularly do something to tidy up and clean your home, eventually it's going to become a real problem.

Counteract a negative interaction as soon as possible. Okay, this is my contribution to the theory. Experience tells me that a negative interaction allowed to stew and fester for too long may actually need *more* than five counterbalancing positive interactions to remedy it. Address and correct little frictions as soon as possible.

It's not symmetrical. If only one part of a pair feels that something was a negative interaction, then it is. In other words, one person perceiving negativity is enough. That also means it goes the other way—both parties need to agree that an interaction feels positive for it to be so. Makes sense, but it's easy to forget in the heat of the moment.

Maintain the effort over time. Finally, Dr. Gottman's research suggests that successful relationships not only follow a 5:1 ratio during conflicts but actually aim for a 20:1 ratio outside of conflict. This means that couples should actively interact positively with their partner in everyday life. The higher the ratio, the less damage a minor argument or misunderstanding will cause if/when it happens.

There Is No "Neutral"
So much for the theory. Let's see, however, what this all looks like in real-life. What exactly counts as an "interaction," anyway? In our previous example it was an argument or disagreement that registered as a negative interaction, but realistically, **negative interactions are often much smaller and more subtle than this.**

Imagine that you've connected with an interesting person in your hobby group and you're getting to know one another. Whenever you spend time together, though, you notice you always feel a little tired and irritable afterward. There is nothing very obvious to put your finger on, but when you pay attention, you notice many tiny things: They complain a lot, they often second-guess you or behave in a way that suggests they doubt or disregard what you say, they tend to automatically and subtly argue with you, even about little things that don't matter, they don't always pay attention or listen, and once or twice they've half ignored you as they checked their phone during a conversation.

Now, this person may be extremely intelligent and interesting and have a lot in common with you. They may occasionally give you compliments, and they keep reaching out to make plans to meet. And yet, after just a few months, you pull the plug on the friendship and drift apart, feeling a little guilty but also relieved.

What happened? That's simple: You had a buildup of negative interactions that were never quite balanced by enough positive. If you imagine any relationship as a kind of bank account, you made too many withdrawals without investing anything back in, and quickly got overdrawn. Eventually, it's no longer worth it.

Of course, it's always possible that *we* are the ones who are unwittingly alienating and offending people by being too negative. While nobody likes to think that they could be this person, I want to tell you that it is very easy to slip into habitual patterns of negativity without realizing it. Try to remind yourself that in relationships of any kind, **there is no "neutral" moment—either you are growing and strengthening rapport, or you're weakening it**. If you neglect or place strain on your connection, it may survive for a while, but only if you've got some positive interactions in the bank already, so to speak.

A negative interaction is not just a small amount of damage done to the connection or the other person directly, however. Think about the person who is looking for love but spends every first date complaining about how bad the people on their previous dates were. Or consider the person who, having just become new friends with someone, immediately makes them their impromptu therapist, sharing every last deep dark secret and emotionally overwrought memory of childhood trauma. Gossip, complaining, and nitpicking may also eat away at the foundation of a relationship.

The great thing about Gottman's theory is that it actually makes it easy to swing the balance in a positive direction:

- Be thoughtful and considerate and do something nice and unexpected for them
- Offer a sincere compliment that will really mean something to them
- Show that you remember important details they've shared with you
- Remember their birthday and important dates
- Choose gifts that they'll actually like
- Actively thank them for things they do for you and express your gratitude
- Praise them in a group where they can overhear you
- Send them a link to an interesting article or book, a cute picture, or a joke to brighten their day

- Be mindful of their limitations and boundaries, and proactively respect them without being asked
- Do something to lighten their load, like taking on a small chore
- Pay one hundred percent undivided attention to them when they're speaking
- Validating them, i.e., "that makes sense"
- Check in with them after important or stressful events to see how they are
- Asking thoughtful and meaningful questions
- Invite them out somewhere or plan an activity
- Take care of them when they're sick or struggling with something
- Be genuinely interested in their opinion on something
- If it's appropriate, give hugs or other signs of affection
- Deliberately choose not to make a big deal out of their shortcomings or mistakes
- Introduce them to someone they may benefit from knowing
- Immediately apologize when you're in the wrong without making excuses
- Give positive feedback, support, and advice (when solicited)
- Make the effort to respond in good time to messages
- Tell them directly that you appreciate them!

When I moved to a new area after college and was trying to make new friends, without knowing it I jeopardized a lot of potential new friendships before they had even begun. Some friends of work colleagues would invite me out somewhere, or someone would reach out and try to strike up a conversation with me. Most of the time I'd respond, but occasionally I'd feel too lazy to make the effort and would turn down the invitation or make an excuse for not having responded sooner. My reasoning was that they weren't *really* my friends, so it wouldn't matter too much.

The trouble is, I was starting off any potential connection with those people completely on the wrong foot—that is, with a negative interaction. From their perspective, there was very little reason to try again or to do the work necessary to offset my non-committal laziness! Once I understood how unrealistic my position was, I changed my strategy and deliberately put *more* effort into those early relationships, even though they were still just technically strangers. I imagined that I was starting from zero and the only way to get things going was to somehow get five positive interactions going.

Once I started thinking this way, I gradually began to make (and keep!) more friends. These days, if I'm feeling lazy and antisocial, my friends will understand, but that's only because we have a history and enough positive interactions banked. I no longer wait for other people to make the "first move," or assume that just because a conversation ended a little weirdly on an awkward note, that nothing can be done. I take it on myself to do whatever it takes to keep contributing those positive interactions.

The Trust Equation

The last time you were in the market for a dentist, how did you eventually choose from the many potential professionals in our area? You might have done some research, looked at some websites or online reviews, or considered some word-of-mouth recommendations. But in the end, who did you most trust with your dental health? Maybe the unprofessional-looking fonts on one dentist's website made you suspicious; perhaps the cheesy glamour shot on another dentist's profile made him look vain and self-absorbed. What was it about the conversation with the receptionist that made you decide a certain company wasn't for you?

Without knowing it, you were likely doing your own mental calculations, appraising just how much you could trust these individuals. It turns out that perceptions of trust are not just important when it comes to choosing healthcare or buying a service, but in decision-making about who to be friends with, who to love, and who to tell our secrets to.

In this chapter, we're pulling all these hidden, intuitive decisions out from the unconscious and making them more obvious so that we can make sure we're not accidentally conveying an image of untrustworthiness to others. While trust itself isn't something that can be quantified easily, there is some research to suggest that the elements it's composed of can be measured.

The trust equation is a handy formula introduced by Charles H. Green, co-author of the book *The Trusted Advisor*, with David Maister and Robert M. Galford. This formula may be the most complicated in the book, but there's a reason for that. Trust is very, very special. Difficult to build, easy to break, trust is something you cannot shortcut or fake.

Green's formula provides a practical framework for understanding and building trust in professional relationships, but I think there's a lot to learn when it comes to friendships, romantic relationships, and those with family members. The formula tells us the ingredients needed to build someone's trust in another person. These ingredients are: credibility, reliability, intimacy, and self-orientation. These elements contribute to an individual's trustworthiness, which can be calculated using the formula:

Trustworthiness = (Credibility + Reliability + Intimacy) ÷ Self-Orientation

Credibility relates to what a person says and their expertise, knowledge, and conviction in their subject matter. How credible someone is refers to how believable and convincing they are. This is, broadly, about the WORDS.

Reliability refers to what a person does, including their ability to keep promises, meet deadlines, and go the extra mile to fulfill the commitments they've made. This is about the ACTIONS.

Intimacy involves the emotional aspect of trust, focusing on the more subjective feelings of safety and security in the relationship, confidentiality, and the belief that personal values and boundaries will be respected. This is about your FEELINGS when around them.

These three factors all go toward cultivating that feeling of trust one person has for another, or to put it another way, that second person's trustworthiness. The fourth factor, however, works to undermine the combined total of these trust-building elements, represented by the division in the equation.

Self-orientation refers to the person's focus, whether it is primarily on themselves or on others. Low self-orientation indicates a focus on others' needs and concerns. High self-orientation needs little explanation—it's when we perceive that someone may be self-absorbed, a little vain, or primarily looking out for themselves.

Trustworthiness is influenced by these elements, and increasing credibility, reliability, and intimacy while reducing self-orientation is how trustworthy you will appear to other people. No, this doesn't automatically imply that they'll like you, find you entertaining, or want to marry you, but being trusted is certainly a non-negotiable first step that you won't get far without!

As the formula shows, even a considerable total score on the top half of the equation can be undermined by a too-large self-orientation—or at least by what others perceive to be self-orientation. Likewise, you can be exceptionally credible, but lack that warmth and intimacy, bringing the total score down. This equation is great because it can help you identify exactly where you are (possibly) falling short.

How do you know whether others trust you or not? People generally demonstrate their trust of you if:

- They openly share their feelings with you, expecting that you won't judge them
- They assume that sensitive information will be kept confidential
- They are not too defensive about their insecurities or vulnerabilities in your presence
- They proactively seek your advice and judgment on important things
- They comfortably rely on you for support and assistance, and happily expect that you'll follow through on commitments and promises

Of course, people may *not* trust you and do little to outwardly show that fact. Your best way forward is to cultivate your overall trustworthiness anyway!

Applying The Trust Equation

Imagine the barista at your local coffee shop, where you get coffee most days. The barista scores around eight out of ten for credibility because they work in a good café and serve great coffee. They're credible and believable in the sense that you really do expect to get a good coffee from them—as you have before. Maybe they lose a few points because they seem a little on the young side, and you wonder just how much experience they have.

They may score nine out of ten for reliability since they consistently provide the coffee you order and have only once gotten things muddled in all the months you've gone to that café. In terms of intimacy, they make you and the other customers feel comfortable and welcome by being friendly, so they get a seven out of ten. Their self-orientation score is low at two out of ten because when you encounter them, they are focused exclusively on serving others. In fact, you have never seen them do anything other than serve coffee!

Applying the trust equation:

Trustworthiness = (Credibility + Reliability + Intimacy) ÷ Self-Orientation
Trustworthiness = (8 + 9 + 7) / 2
Trustworthiness = 24 / 2
Trustworthiness = 12

The barista's trustworthiness is calculated as twelve, indicating that they are considered quite trustworthy based on these factors. **The highest possible score is thirty, but this is unlikely to be met by mere mortals; anything above eight or nine is pretty good.**

Now, you've probably spied the limitations and caveats of the trust equation. You might assign the barista a twelve *when it comes to making coffee.* Do you trust him to give you a root canal, however? Would you trust him to date your sister? Would you trust him to keep your secrets or pay back a loan of one thousand dollars? As you can see, trust is often very context dependent.

It's often easier to come across as trustworthy in more limited, superficial, or professional contexts, because the social demands are fewer and more clearly defined. We only need to trust a barista to the extent that he'll make us good coffee. Trustworthiness in other areas, however, is naturally more complicated.

You can try out this equation for yourself right now. Pick a handful of friends, acquaintances, or family members and do a quick overall calculation for your perception of their trustworthiness. It can be a fascinating exercise; sometimes we have a gut feeling for why we're a little suspicious of someone, but working through an equation like this can give us real insight into why we feel that way. Of course, the real insight comes when you understand that other people are making their own hidden calculations of your trustworthiness, too!

I want to finish by revisiting my earlier example—the one in which I was being a little flaky with potential new friends in the area I'd just moved to. What might my trustworthiness score look like from their perspective?

Applying the trust equation:

Trustworthiness = (Credibility + Reliability + Intimacy) ÷ Self-Orientation

How credible was I? Not clear. They didn't really know me.
How reliable was I? Not very!
How intimate—in other words, how good—did I make them feel? This is also an unknown.
How self-oriented must I have appeared? Also not clear, but cancelling last minute would not have looked good, so this may well have been the highest score in the whole equation.

So, we have:

Trustworthiness = (? + 3 + ?) / 5
Trustworthiness = ?

How do we calculate that? What is *your* impression when you look at that equation? With too many unknowns, low scores of good stuff, and a considerable score of bad stuff, is it any surprise people weren't keen to keep reaching out to me? Take it as a given that too many question marks will never inspire trust.

The truth of the matter was that I was just being lazy (and maybe a little shy, if I'm honest), but unfortunately shyness and reluctance to engage can easily be interpreted as self-orientation, too. What I'm driving at is that trust and the "positive interactions" covered in the last section overlap one another. And, remembering that there is no "neutral" in human relationships, it's worth being aware that an absence of information is often felt to be a teeny tiny negative.

If I do what I can to fill in those unknowns, even moderate scores will make a better impression than the one above. This ties in with the Friendship Formula we looked at in the very first chapter:

Friendship = Proximity + Frequency + Duration + Intensity

Trust follows a not dissimilar principle. The more opportunities we create to make ourselves feel like a known quantity, the more familiar we will seem and the easier it will be to trust us.

The Elements of a Good Apology

Even the most robust and long-standing friendship can crumble if, after a perceived slight, an apology is not forthcoming. While many people will be happy to forgive and forget a transgression if someone is genuinely sorry, the failure to apologize (or apologize correctly) can quickly become its own offense, often perceived as even worse than the original mistake.

How good are you at apologies? If your answer is, "I'm not sure, I've never made one . . ." then you can assume that some practice is in order! If you've been the perfect social genius and managed to cultivate enormous trust and goodwill among your friends, then congratulations. Most of us, though, will put our foot in it sooner or later, and **how we respond to such a situation may make or break that social connection**.

Apologizing is a challenging but essential skill that can be learned. What I've learned is that apologizing well is one of those life skills that everyone assumes is obvious, but people seldom get right. If you think about your own life, you may discover, sadly, that this is true; when last did *you* receive an apology that sincerely helped you move on from the issue and reconnect with the other person?

In a comprehensive study led by Roy Lewicki, six steps to offering a more effective apology were identified. According to Lewicki, apologizing is a rather complex social phenomenon that actually follows identifiable and predictable rules. Apologizing well involves acknowledging your mistakes sincerely, and ironically, it can feel most challenging to offer an apology in precisely those situations where one is most needed.

The study, published in *Negotiation and Conflict Management Research* in 2016, involved 755 participants and examined various elements of effective apologies. An effective apology consists of six key elements. You may smooth over ruffled feathers with an apology that misses a few of these, but your chances of real reconciliation are best when you include them all in a conscious way. Importantly, they are listed in order from most to least effective. The elements are:

- **Acknowledgment of responsibility:** Admitting full fault and taking responsibility for the mistake.
- **Offer to fix the problem:** Demonstrating a commitment to taking action to rectify the damage caused, sometimes called reparations.

- **Expression of regret:** Conveying genuine remorse for the wrongdoing.
- **Explanation of what went wrong:** Providing an explanation for why the offense occurred (depending on the situation, this may be best skipped).
- **Declaration of repentance:** Expressing a commitment to not repeat the mistake, and possibly taking a concrete step toward that commitment.
- **A request for forgiveness:** The least important step and one that can be omitted if necessary.

The most crucial element for an effective apology is the "acknowledgment of responsibility." Even if you tick all the other boxes, an apology missing this important element seriously risks coming across as insincere and may not be accepted.

Has someone ever apologized to you by saying something weaselly like, "I'm sorry you got offended," or, "I'm sorry that happened (all by itself, magically)"? For someone who is feeling hurt and insulted, there is a strong sense of the order of the universe being upset. An apology's first task is to acknowledge that injustice and then hopefully correct it. As soon as you can, admit your part in what happened and avoid blaming someone else (especially the person you're apologizing to!).

The second important element is the "offer of repair," as it shows commitment to rectify the situation. Practice bucketloads of empathy and perspective taking here. Why exactly might the other person be upset? What do they feel right now, and what would most make them feel better?

Three other elements—expression of regret, explanation of what went wrong, and declaration of repentance—are also effective and can be included, but they are not the place to start. Expressing regret is, when you think about it, all about you, so don't dwell too long on how bad you feel, but it may be useful to express how your own actions are perceived as wrong, too.

Similarly, explanations are meant to help the other person understand that something might not have been personal (i.e., a mistake), but be careful that your explanations don't veer into excuses and justifications. Instead, an explanation can sometimes make people feel better if they understand that the harm was not done on purpose, or caused by laziness or oversight rather than a vindictive intention to offend them.

Declaring that you're repentant and won't ever do it again is not a bad thing to include in an apology—provided you really mean it. It goes without saying that if this is a second identical offense, you may not help your cause by making promises not to do it again. Instead, be patient and let your actions speak.

Finally, the least effective element in an apology is "request for forgiveness," as it often serves the apologizer's interests more than the recipient's. Asking outright to be forgiven can make an apology seem more formal and considered, but try not to convey any entitlement to how that person should respond to your apology. You can certainly ask, but what they do after receiving your apology is their business. Even if their reaction seems stubborn and unreasonable to you, and you're not forgiven when you believe you should be, try to let it go.

Before we take a closer look at a great template for an effective apology, let's consider a few key things to avoid.

DON'T wait too long to apologize. As soon as possible after you realize what's happened is best. Don't wait for them to get mad!

DON'T suggest that the other person is overly sensitive, mistaken, or silly for being offended. Don't apologize sarcastically or insincerely—it's worse than no apology at all.

DON'T apologize over and over again. Do it once, well, and then leave it be. You are not required to be repentant for the rest of your life.

Finally, DON'T over- or under-apologize. Match your apology to the size of the infringement (from their perspective, not yours). Give a short, simple apology for a small mistake, and a longer, more formal one for when you've really messed up.

Here are a few examples of apologies that just may do more harm than good:

For example, you were looking after your friend's indoor cat, accidentally left the door open, and the cat ran loose and was run over by a car. Let's say you apologize by saying, "Oh, wow, I'm so sorry Minky died. Please don't be mad at me. She just ran out; it was crazy. I've been up all night just sick with worry about the whole thing. I'm so sorry. This has never happened to me before."

Though the words "I'm sorry" technically appear, this is not even close to a real apology, since it lacks any acknowledgment of responsibility, makes no offer to put things right, and instead of explaining things, resorts to blame (of the cat!) and excuse-making. What's more, it centers your uncomfortable feelings rather than paying attention to theirs. Many people offer "apologies" of this kind and then are surprised when others don't feel reassured. "But I said I was sorry!"

Another example of something that may sound like an apology but isn't is the over-apology. Imagine someone at work steals your project idea and passes it off as their own. It's a little brazen, but it's not a major issue and it happens all the time in your industry. You call them out on it, and they send you an apology email the next day that goes like this:

"I wanted you to know I accept full and total responsibility for my shameful behavior yesterday. I know in my heart that there is nothing on this earth I can do to go back in time and fix what I've broken, but please know that I am wracking my brains trying to find a way to make this right with you, who I have always considered a friend. I deeply regret my actions. I can offer no explanation but my own mortal weakness, of which I am more ashamed than you can know. One thing I can assure you is that as long as I live, I vow never to repeat the same mistake again. I know it's too much to ask that you ever move on from this—you've been through enough already, I know—but one day, maybe, my dearest hope is that you can forgive me and all the many, many ways I fall short of my own standards."

Okay, that was cringeworthy, right? Yet it contained all the elements of a good apology! The problem was it was an apology that was far, far too big for the transgression it was trying to make amends for. A strange thing happens when people make an exaggerated display of contrition—it starts to feel phony and insulting in its own way. Have you ever witnessed a drawn-out and tearful TV apology by a celebrity for some extremely minor offense? What about a multinational company releasing a pages-long public apology for saying the wrong thing on social media? The over-apology is indulgent and irrelevant in those cases where people simply want to know that you know that what happened was wrong, and that it's not going to happen again. The rest is theater!

APOLOGY TEMPLATE

Acknowledgment of Responsibility
"It's my fault"; "I take full responsibility . . ."

Offer of Repair:
"I'll help you by _____"
"I'll fix it by helping you to _____."
"How about I (offer to help in some unrelated way)?"

Expression of Regret:
"I'm so sorry. I regret _____."
"I wish I could take it back, but I can't."

Explanation of What Went Wrong:
"It happened because _____."

Declaration of Repentance:
"It won't happen again because _____."
"I can guarantee that from now on _____."
"I promise _____."

Request for Forgiveness:
"If you can find it in your heart to forgive me, I'd appreciate _____."
"I hope we can move on from this one day."

Example: You double park in the shared lot at your apartment complex, and a neighbor gets a little annoyed. You say, "Oops, I've double parked—that's one hundred percent on me! I'll immediately move my car to a proper parking spot. I'm so sorry; that was very thoughtless of me. It happened because I was in a hurry and not paying attention. It won't happen again."

Example: Your best friend ends up in the hospital, and you make excuses to not visit him, choosing instead to avoid his calls. He is discharged before you get to visit him, but he's upset. Your apology may sound like this: "Ben, this is difficult for me to say, but I've been a total jerk. I know that. This is my fault, and I'm sorry. I know you're out of the hospital already, but can I take you out somewhere, just you and me, my treat? I know it doesn't make up for how I let you down, and I feel bad about that. Since my dad died, I guess I've been really uneasy around hospitals and was putting off coming to see you just because I didn't want to face being there again. But I can promise you I won't ditch you like that again. What do you say, will you let me take you out for a drink or something?"

Both of these examples contain most of the crucial elements and are appropriate to the context. In the second, more serious one, we see that the request for forgiveness component can take a more subtle form as a tentative request to simply repair the connection. Often, there is no real way to make repairs or undo the damage done, but you can go a long way to reconciliation by making a gesture that shows that you want to re-establish trust and rapport with that person . . . even if it has to be in an unrelated way. Remember the trust bank account and the importance of positive interactions? Consider an apology a very important positive interaction that is meant primarily to bring you out of relational debt and get you on the right track again!

Summary

- Dr. Gottman's "5:1 rule" suggests that **a healthy relationship follows the ratio of 5:1, with AT LEAST five positive interactions for every negative one.** This guideline reminds us that relationships need to be maintained over time.

- Criticism, defensiveness, contempt, and stonewalling are negative interactions, while positive interactions include support, validation, listening, affection, and so on. To counteract the negative effects of a single negative interaction during conflict, you need to consciously follow up with at least five positive interactions.

- Negative interactions are normal, but how you respond to them is your responsibility. Negative interactions are often much smaller and more subtle than this. There is no neutral—either an interaction helps rapport, or it hinders it.

- Charles Green's formula for trust is **Trustworthiness = (Credibility + Reliability + Intimacy) ÷ Self-Orientation.**

- Credibility relates to how believable and convincing they are (WORDS). Reliability refers to their ability to keep promises and fulfill the commitments they've made (ACTIONS). Intimacy involves the emotional aspect of trust, and the belief that personal values and boundaries will be respected (FEELINGS). Self-orientation refers to the person's focus, whether it is primarily on themselves or on others. Low self-orientation indicates a focus on others' needs and concerns, and leads to more trust.

- The highest possible score is thirty, but anything above eight or nine is pretty good. Remember also that trust is context dependent, and that too many unknowns often inspire mistrust.
- According to Roy Lewicki, the best apologies contain a few key elements, in order of importance: **acknowledgment of responsibility, offer to fix the problem, expression of regret, explanation of what went wrong, declaration of repentance, and a request for forgiveness**.
- Don't wait too long to apologize, don't over-apologize, and don't repeatedly apologize. Carefully match the apology to the person receiving it, the size of the offense, and the context.

Chapter 5: What's My Exit Strategy?

The XYZ Formula for Assertive Communication

So far, we have considered a set of communication skills that span the life cycle of a social interaction. First, you cross that chasm between you and another unknown person by gradually increasing proximity, intensity, etc., you reach out with small talk, and you find good ways to introduce yourself and start to build familiarity.

Then, while getting to know a person, you practice the fundamental communication skill— listening—and through that you develop your ability to empathize and switch into perspectives that are not your own. By connecting emotionally, you find that you are

143

able to form better friendships, speak so that people really understand you, and even master the art of persuasion, storytelling, and being generally fun to be around.

When things *don't* go so well, however, you need to be able to zoom out and think about the bigger picture and how to keep the balance between positive and negative interactions, build trust over time, and know exactly what to do when you mess up so that balance and harmony are restored again.

Our final chapter extends this theme of what to do when communication breaks down a little, a misunderstanding appears, or there is outright conflict and friction. First, it is a myth that socially intelligent people get along with everyone all the time. If you are a human being, at some point you *will* find yourself experiencing some kind of tension with another human being. Socially intelligent people don't experience less of this kind of conflict; they are simply better at managing it when it does crop up.

Knowing how to sincerely and effectively apologize when you've damaged the social connection is a skill worth its weight in gold. But of course, sometimes you're the one who feels affronted, or as though your boundaries are being pushed on or broken outright. If you are a close follower of Gottman's 5:1 relationship ratio principle, then you give yourself ample opportunity to make minor course corrections in your relationships so that small niggles and issues never get the chance to become big serious ones.

The XYZ formula for assertive communication is a structured way to express your thoughts, feelings, and needs in a clear and assertive manner. It helps you effectively communicate your concerns while respecting the feelings and needs of the other person involved. Basically, it's an approach that helps you navigate choppy social waters with as much grace as possible. **The goal is simple: Interact in such a way that both your rights and their rights are respected**. **This ultimately preserves the relationship so that it can survive conflict.**

Using empathy, listening, and an intention to connect emotionally, you are able to express your own needs clearly while allowing yourself to hear and accommodate the needs of the other person. The desired end is that the conflict dissolves while your connection remains intact.

For many people, "assertive communication" sounds a little scary. It is, however, an essential tool in your social toolkit and is in fact one of the kindest, most mature ways you can interact with someone. Let's briefly revise the different communication styles:

Passive: Here, you place other people's needs and rights above your own, or even instead of your own. It may seem superficially kind of polite, but it's dishonest on a fundamental level and will only lead to resentment and misunderstanding in the long run. For example, you watch as your friend marches into your pristine home with muddy boots, ruining your expensive white carpets. You say nothing because you don't want to make them feel uncomfortable. Well, they aren't . . . but you are!

Aggressive: The opposite, where you put your own needs and rights ahead of other peoples', or even seek your own ends at the expense of theirs. Sure, you may be honest and direct, but you risk causing offense and damaging that social connection. You may show them *and yourself* a lack of respect. For example, the woman at the checkout fumbles with your grocery bill, and you yell at her to pay better attention, and ask if she's brain damaged or something. She may indeed pay attention and do better . . . but at what expense?

Passive aggressive: Arguably the worst of all worlds since nobody's needs are met. You are unable to ask for what you want outright so you hint and suggest and guilt and imply, all the while trying to manipulate the other person into doing what you want them to do. Contrary to what many people think, passive aggression is *not* polite—it's disrespectful and profoundly damages relationships. For example, someone has a need to be cared for and loved when they're ill, but instead of asking for that, they casually say to their friends, "I wonder what it's like to have people you can depend on. Hmm . . . guess I'll never know!"

Assertive, active, and healthy: This is communication that is direct, honest, appropriate, and respectful. It respects and balances the needs of both. Nobody is placed above or below—communication is done with the intention of equality. Asserting boundaries, making your needs and limits clear, and negotiating with others is not mean—it's sometimes the only way to reach harmony. Let's revisit each of the previous examples and communicate them in a healthier way.

"Hey, friend, I'm so glad you're here. Make yourself at home! Can I get you a drink? Oh, and we take our shoes off here. These carpets are hell to clean!" (Acknowledges and respects your friend's right to be different from you, their right to make an innocent mistake, and their right to feel comfortable and welcome in your home. It also asserts your own right to have your things respected.)

"I can see that the error with my bill is not your fault. That's okay. But you've overcharged my card. Can we call the manager to fix this?" (Acknowledges and respects the right of the cashier to be spoken to with dignity, as well as your right to not be charged unfairly or inconvenienced by someone else's mistake.)

"Guys, I've been feeling so down since I got pneumonia. Can I ask for a little extra TLC or something today? Maybe you can come over and we can all have chicken soup and watch a movie?" (Acknowledging your own need and right to want a little affection, but also respecting your friends' needs to not be mind readers and guess what you want!)

So, let's clear one thing up: Assertive communication, respecting your own boundaries, and being clear about your limits and needs are *healthy* and *kind*. So long as you can strike the balance between your needs and rights and theirs, you will likely find a sane, mature way through any conflict without creating too much damage or drama.

Let's take a look at the components of the XYZ formula:

X—This represents the **emotion** you are feeling. It's essential to start by identifying and expressing your emotions, and possibly how they connect to your needs. This helps the other person understand the impact of their actions on you.

Y—This part explains the specific **behavior** or action of the other person that is resulting in your emotion. It's crucial to be clear and specific about the behavior or situation that is bothering you, but without actively blaming or insulting the other person.

Z—This component refers to the situation or **context** in which the behavior occurred. It helps set the context and provides additional information to the other person.

After expressing X, Y, and Z, you're not done; from there proceed to the second part:

"I would like"—This is where you communicate your needs and desires regarding the situation. It's important to be clear and specific about what you would like to happen to address the issue. There should be a clear thread linking X, Y, and Z, and this should lead directly to the request you make.

The XYZ* Formula for Assertive Communication			
I feel X emotion	when you do Y specific behavior	in situation Z specific situation	and I would like what you want
I feel disrespected	when you're on your phone at night	and I'm trying to sleep	I would like you to text instead of talking after 10 pm.
I feel uncomfortable	when you bring someone home for the night	and you don't talk with me about it first	I would like to know your plans ahead of time so I can make other plans if I choose.
I feel anxious	when we don't discuss the progress on my research	at our weekly meetings	I'd like us to reserve some time each week to discuss it.

In each of the examples above, you are able to communicate assertively in just one or two sentences. Be respectful, confident, and direct. Keep your words clear, controlled, and calm. Practice as much compassion as you can for the other person and their perspective while remembering to maintain the same attitude to your own wants and needs, too. Assertive conversations can sometimes be uncomfortable or difficult, but they are almost always more effective in the long run than being dishonest, indirect, disrespectful, or avoidant.

The XYZ formula is extremely simple, but the way it plays out in real life is nuanced. Consider, for example, the following:

"It drives me crazy when you leave your filthy dishes everywhere."
"When you don't do the washing up, it clutters the kitchen and makes it difficult for me to cook. Could we work on a schedule or something to make sure the washing up is done every day?"

The first is likely to elicit defensiveness and excuses from the other person; the second is far more likely to lead to a situation where everyone is relatively happy. If our rule was: interact in such a way that everyone's rights are respected, and preserve the relationship so that it can survive conflict, then the first will probably fail.

The XYZ formula is great for everyday social snags, but you might need to expand it somewhat for bigger conflicts. When expressing some kind of grievance or trying to assert more serious boundaries, try following these steps.

1. Recognize the issue or situation. Keep to one issue at a time.
2. Describe the situation as neutrally and objectively as you can. Use language that the other person would agree with. Avoid blaming and shaming. Be specific and try not to leap to conclusions or make assumptions about what the other person thinks and feels or what they intended. It's the difference between "you're disrespectful" and "I don't feel my needs are being respected."
3. Tell them how you feel. After the facts and details are quickly covered, be honest about your concerns, preferably using "I" statements. "I would feel so much more

relaxed if you turned up on time" is better than "You're always late."

4. Check in with their perspective, be mindful of their position, and ask about their needs. Give them a chance to respond and share just as you have.

5. Finally, make a reasonable request for a behavior you'd like from them. You can be clear about the positive outcomes that will occur if they are able to do this behavior, and even emphasize how it's likely to be mutually beneficial. In other words, you want to end the conversation with a clear route out of the problem and toward something better. Without this step your assertive communication risks coming across as mere complaining or fault-finding. Be specific and reasonable in what you're asking.

"Yesterday I told the kids that they couldn't watch TV, but then you said they could, and neither of them ended up doing their homework. I believe it's happened a few times before, too, where you and I did not present a united front with the kids. I feel pretty frustrated because I got a message from the kids' teacher about the homework not being done, but I also feel upset that my authority is not being respected. What do you think?" (Waits to hear some reaction and the other person's perspective.) "Okay, I hear you. That makes sense. Moving forward, do you think we could both spend some time tomorrow ironing out the details together, something we can both agree on? Then when we set rules for the kids, we're on the same page."

The Best Way to End Conversations

What better way to end our social skills journey than to consider endings themselves and how to best navigate them. You may spend so much time worrying about and planning for the initial stages of a social interaction that you're completely caught off-guard when it comes to wrapping things up and saying goodbye.

But goodbyes are just as important as hellos, partly because if done right, they lay the groundwork for a comfortable start for the *next* conversation. Ending on a high note and keeping the door open for further positive interactions is a skill all on its own. Social interactions, just like the broader relationships they're a part of, have a natural life cycle. Some of us can get awkward around ending a chat because we subtly interpret it as a kind of failure. But all conversations—even great ones—must come to an end at some point. The first question is, when?

A big clue that your conversation is getting a bit long in the tooth is if you notice longer and longer periods of silence. You'll know when a silence is a natural, comfortable one, and when it's getting awkward. Not to worry; this doesn't mean that you're boring or that they are! If you proactively end the conversation at this point, before it becomes very obviously uncomfortable, then you have the strongest chance of the other person finding you as interesting next time as they did in the beginning of this conversation. Basically, when in doubt, keep things shorter, not longer.

Now, what about *how* to end a conversation once you've decided it's time is up? It might sound strange, but there is actually accumulated behavioral evidence regarding the art of concluding conversations. One of the first empirical studies was conducted at Purdue University in 1973. A research team took eighty participants and divided them into pairs, instructing them to do a semi-structured interview with one another. They told one party, however, to end the conversation as quickly as possible after all the questions were answered, while leaving the other to do what they felt natural.

When they analyzed these conversation endings, the team discovered the same repeating patterns and the same elements occurring in the way people wound up the interaction. They found that people tended to offer verbal reinforcement and a courtesy warning that an end was coming. You know the kind of thing: saying, "All right ..." or, "Well then ..." and leaving it open so the other person could instigate the final few words themselves. An effective goodbye seems to rest on a mutual acknowledgement that the process is slightly negative, and so we agree to buffer and mitigate the situation with some kind, supportive words.

Stuart Albert at the University of Pennsylvania and Suzanne Kessler of SUNY-Purchase actually created their own special formula for effectively terminating a social encounter, including the following elements:

- Content Summary Statement
- Justification
- Positive Affect Statement
- Continuity
- Well-Wishing

$$[S_c] \rightarrow [J] \rightarrow \begin{bmatrix} P \\ S_a \end{bmatrix} \rightarrow [C] \rightarrow [W]$$

To put that "formula" into words gives us this generic conversation-ending format:

"Okay, well, we talked about what we needed to talk about [content summary statement], and I have a valid reason for ending our conversation [justification]. I enjoyed and appreciated our conversation [positive affect statement]. Let me reassure you that we will repeat it sometime in the future [continuity]. Take care, be happy, go well [well-wishing]."

Content Summary Statement: This involves summarizing the main topics or points discussed during the conversation. This gives you both a feeling of closure and completion.

Justification: Providing a reason for ending the conversation, which may include other commitments or responsibilities. Naturally, you want this to be as genuine and believable as possible. While you're also perfectly in your rights to want to end a conversation just because you want to end it, consider it a social taboo to ever say so.

Positive Affect Statement: Expressing genuine positive feelings about the interaction, indicating enjoyment or appreciation. Some of the negative feelings from the end of an interaction can come from subtle fears that it may end the relationship—this component is a reassurance otherwise.

Continuity: Suggesting or planning for future interactions to maintain the relationship. You're in effect saying "till next time" rather than "goodbye!"

Well-Wishing: Conveying well-wishes or positive sentiments as you part ways. Think about this final social gesture as a little bow you put on the conversation as you wrap it up and set it aside completely.

Without these five elements, the end of a conversation can be quite a vulnerable and fraught time, and can very quickly create some bad feelings. Ending too abruptly or drawing things out too long may sour the entire interaction that came before. In some ways, a good conversation is a little like a plane trip— it's the takeoff and landing that are most important!

Zombie Conversations

What about if you're in a conversation with someone who just won't take a hint?

Not everyone agrees when the conversation has run its course, and people may have very different ideas about when exactly to end it. Many of the researchers in this area have identified that people have all sorts of ways of wriggling out of conversations that feel like they just won't die, from polite and not-so-polite hints, to changing the topic, to making excuses, to getting the help of a third party to rescue you, to becoming unresponsive, to just plain being rude. Finding that sweet spot between socially acceptable and effective can be challenging!

First, the bad news: you are probably not as good at noticing when to end a conversation as you think you are. Many studies find that, when reporting back on conversations with other participants, people often feel that their conversations had gone on too long, rather than wishing they had gone on longer. If everyone tends to feel that conversations could have ended earlier, this strongly suggests we could all learn to be better at recognizing our conversation partner's fatigue and desire to end things!

Not-so-obvious signs include:

- A sudden and abrupt change in body language, restlessness, or subtle signs of fatigue (yawning, stretching, glancing around, shifting weight from one leg to the other).
- Expressions of how you must want the conversation to end. For example, "Oh, well, I'm sure you've got somewhere to be, so I won't keep you . . ."
- Attempts to rope others into the conversation.
- Failing to expand on a thread and instead continuing to try to conclude the topic. "Oh, well! It's a crazy world, huh? Anyway . . ."
- A question or comment about what you plan to do when the conversation is over (beware—this is often not an invitation to

continue talking; the person is trying to segue away from the current conversation). "So, whereabouts did you park? Must be time to pick the kids up from school soon?"

- Talking about the conversation in past tense. "This has been such a nice catch-up!"
- Thanking you for something—this is a roundabout way of summarizing the conversation, which is a roundabout way of saying that it's over. "Thanks for giving me her email address. I'll let you know what she says."

In other words, if you catch other people making hints toward any of the five components mentioned above, be alert that they may be signaling that they're ready to close things off. If the context warrants it, if the other person is extremely polite or passive, or simply if you don't know each other well, it might be quite difficult to pinpoint this moment exactly. Again, it's better to quit while you're ahead!

Now, be prepared for the fact that if you're the one finding yourself in a zombie conversation that won't die and stay dead, you're going to have to put in a bit more effort. If you offer a conversation-ending phrase that follows the formula above, most people will understand and graciously follow through with saying goodbye. Occasionally, however, it won't take, and you'll have to double down.

The best part of the formula to repeat, and repeat more strongly, is the justification part. If a person doesn't take a subtle hint, you will need to steadily be more and more obvious until they do. For various reasons, some people are quite literal and may not be all that good at reading the signs. Others might genuinely fear the conversation ending and desperately try to keep it going even though they have registered that you'd like it to end. In both cases, you'll need to find a way to exit with as much grace and compassion as you can. Be blunt but respectful: "Thank you, Grandpa, but I really must go now, or I'll miss my train. Goodbye! I'll talk to you tomorrow." Literally say the word goodbye. Then, follow up with a very clear and obvious nonverbal signal, like leaving the room, giving them a hug, and walking away, or turning your body to face another direction.

If you find yourself falling victim to a conversational narcissist who is talking and talking and won't let you go, then feel free to interrupt and hastily make your excuses. In my experience, a little bluntness in these cases is often preferable to enduring a conversation that will only create resentment and boredom. If a person is not aware enough to notice your discomfort, they probably won't be aware enough to notice your slight rudeness, either!

Ghosting, fading, and drifting away . . .

As you remember that assertive communication is about respecting others' needs without compromising your own, I'm sure you're starting to see that the rules for ending conversations can also be understood as rules for ending relationships more broadly. You may communicate perfectly, listen well, and be as mature and empathetic as you possibly can be .. . and yet still not quite connect with someone. That's okay!

Social skills make interaction with flawed human beings easier, but it can't make it perfect and risk-free. Two people may dare to try to connect and still find that, for whatever reason, it just doesn't work. When I was a recovering loner and card-carrying shy person, I used to take this sort of thing very personally, believing that a failed friendship was a mistake or something to be ashamed of. As we wrap up this chapter, I want to assure you: It's not possible (or desirable) to click with every person you meet. You don't have to like or agree with or even understand everyone you meet, and the same is true for them. If it were that easy, we wouldn't prize real friendships when we found them, right?

You are entitled to move on from any kind of relationship if the other person doesn't acknowledge your reasonably asserted boundaries, if you don't feel respected or listened to, or if your needs are consistently going unmet. You can end any social connection if there is a lack of empathy and understanding, or if there are just too many accumulating negative interactions. You can also move on simply because, well, you're not getting much from it.

Just as there is an ideal way to start up a new social interaction, however, there is an ideal way to end it, whether it's a new romantic relationship, a casual friendship, or a situation with a close family member. Here are a few things to consider:

You can be compassionate right till the end. You don't have to make them wrong or yourself wrong to end things. Be as kind and considerate as you can.

Ghosting is not the end of the world. Extremely casual and tenuous connections don't require a big formal breakup speech, so don't feel too bad about slowly fading out. That said, outright ignoring people who repeatedly try to get in touch with you is plain cruel.

Use the conversation-ending formula. Say goodbye in a considerate and positive way, including a content summary statement, justification, positive affect statement, continuity statement, and well-wishing to finish. "We've been spending a lot of time together, but I'm afraid I need to focus a bit more on finishing my studies for the time being. It's been great getting to know you, and I'll see you around campus now and then, I'm sure. Take care of yourself, okay?"

Ending things is never, ever easy, but there are certainly ways to get through it that soften some of the sting. If you are ever on the receiving end of this kind of communication, be considerate and polite in return—honesty and forthrightness is a rare thing in the world, so be grateful when someone has the courage to tell you where they stand.

People are amazing. There are billions and billions of them on the earth, and each one is completely unique. Bafflingly, many people feel more alone now than they ever have perhaps in the course of human history. I'm not a historian and won't venture an explanation for why modern humans find it so difficult and stressful to connect socially (I'm sure you have some solid theories of your own), but what I do know is that people are built to connect, and with practice, it does become easier and more natural.

One big aha moment for me was realizing that I didn't *have to* remain socially isolated. Even the shyest, most awkward, or most socially inept among us can learn the skills required to connect more seamlessly with those around us. It just takes a little effort, patience, and the willingness to believe that you can do it. Whoever you are, you are not doomed to feel alone, alienated, or trapped in endless conflict with others. If someone like me can do it, then you definitely can!

The theories and principles I've outlined here are a great foundation—but they're just that, a foundation. It's up to you to build on that foundation day after day with small, positive actions that keep your connections to others alive and thriving. Be patient with other people and, most importantly, with yourself. Be slow to offend and quick to forgive. Have a sense of humor about how utterly frustrating we human beings can be . . . and how delightful it is to continually risk getting to know us anyway!

I want to leave you with what I consider one of the best "formulas" to live by in general. *The Yoga Vashista* says, "There is no power greater than right action in the present." I like to think that:

Success = The right mindset + Action

If you adopt a curious, respectful, and compassionate attitude, *and* you consistently take action in the right direction, you cannot help but succeed—I'm sure of it.

Summary

- Socially intelligent people don't experience less of this kind of conflict, they are simply better at managing it. The goal of assertive communication is to interact in such a way that both your rights and the other person's rights are respected. This ultimately preserves the relationship so that it can survive conflict/friction.
- Healthy communication is not passive (putting their needs first) or aggressive (putting your needs first) or passive aggressive (attempting to meet your needs in an underhanded way). Instead, it's clear, honest, direct, appropriate, polite, and respectful.
- The XYZ formula for assertive communication entails **X (the emotion you are feeling), Y (the specific behavior or action of the other person that is resulting in your emotion), and Z (the situation or context)**. End with a polite and reasonable request for the behavior you'd like.
- Avoid blaming, name-calling, or fruitless complaining. Calm compassion and clarity will go far to restoring harmony again.

- All conversations have a life cycle, and even good ones must end. To master the art of ending a conversation, include a content summary statement, a justification, a positive affect statement, a continuity statement, and some well-wishing to end.
- In words, that looks like, "Okay, we talked about what we needed to talk about [content summary statement], and I have a valid reason for ending our conversation [justification]. I enjoyed and appreciated our conversation [positive affect statement]. Let me reassure you that we will repeat it sometime in the future [continuity]. Take care, be happy, go well [well-wishing]."
- Err on the side of a shorter conversation rather than a longer one. If you are trapped in a "zombie conversation," then repeat the justification part again and more obviously, using nonverbal gestures and the actual word "goodbye." Ending relationships more generally can follow a similar format; always be kind and respectful.

Summary Guide

CHAPTER 1: YOU CAN'T MAKE A SECOND FIRST IMPRESSION

- The things we think are important for forming friendships often aren't. Schafer's Friendship Formula goes like this: **Friendship = Proximity + Frequency + Duration + Intensity**.
- Proximity: Proximity simply refers to the physical or social closeness between individuals.
- Frequency: Frequency involves the number of times you come into contact with a person over a given period.
- Duration: Duration is all about the length of time spent together during each interaction.
- Intensity: Finally, this refers to the depth of the interactions and the emotional or psychological connection created during those interactions. Intensity and depth, then, are closely connected to the needs people meet for one another—needs that may grow stronger or weaker over time.
- Schafer's formula shows you that each of these special ingredients can offset the other. Try to understand where you are with the people in your network, and the next steps you might take on the road from stranger to friend. Place your efforts and

attentions on things that genuinely will influence your ability to form friendships, focusing on the formula components in order. Be patient—it takes time.

- When it comes to socializing, we have to start small. Small talk is what allows big talk. It may seem trivial and unimportant, but it's essential for effective communication. If small talk is small, it lowers risk and brings down that barrier to enter into conversation.

- The small talk formula is **answer the question**, **provide one to two lines of additional detail**, **and pass the turn**.

- The perfect self-introduction follows this formula: **Your perfect personal introduction = Present + Past + Future**.

- The formula for introducing others is: **Introduction for another person = Their name + An interesting fact about them + Something to connect them to the other person**.

CHAPTER 2: HOW TO BE A HUMAN MIRROR (AND EVERYONE LOVES MIRRORS)

- Being a good conversationalist has very little to do with how interesting, impressive, sexy, or intelligent you are. Instead, a good conversationalist understands that their first duty is not to talk, but to listen. **Good**

conversation = Forty-three percent talking + Fifty-seven percent listening (approximately!)

- Adopt an attitude of playfulness, curiosity, and generosity, and treat others like they're the most important people in the world.
- Give conversations time and space by allowing the occasional silence. Show genuine interest and ask questions that actively demonstrate your listening and deep comprehension. The goal of conversation is almost always to meet an emotional need, so listen for the hidden emotional content of what the other person is saying. Finally, avoid continually switching the focus back to yourself (i.e., shift responses) and offer more support responses.
- Active listening is just that—active. It's something you do. Reflective listening involves paying respectful attention to the content and emotions conveyed in someone's communication, whether their need is for validation, vindication, guidance, attention, soothing, advice, a reality check, or simply a kind and attentive audience to confirm that they're not alone. Simply listening can make it easier for others to understand themselves.
- **Reflective response = Tentative check + Feeling + Connection**

- There are four main subtasks in the act of empathy: perspective taking, nonjudgment, emotional literacy, and "feeling with" people, i.e., having empathy.
- Try to subtly communicate, "Hey, I'm here, and I'm listening. I care about you, and I care about what you're saying. You matter and what you're feeling is important. Tell me more." Don't make assumptions, and pay attention to your non-verbal communication, too. There are three types of empathy. **Genuine empathy = Thought + Feeling + Action.** Ideally, all three types are required, each building on the next.

CHAPTER 3: CONNECTING UNDERNEATH THE SURFACE

- Social connection is something we all need for our sense of meaning, purpose, and well-being in life. The goal of any social interaction is to meet these needs, not to convince, persuade, win, or impress others. It's not enough to construct faultless premises, withstand counterarguments, and persuade your listeners to accept your position instead of theirs. Being logically robust in your communications with others is necessary but not sufficient—you have to include emotion, too.

- **Persuasive Communication = (Premises + Conclusion) Emotion.** Your overall effectiveness as a communicator depends on your argument *multiplied by* the emotional connection you're making with the other person. Understand the "facts" but also people's experience of the facts.

- Communicating effectively requires empathy. If you understand what the other person is feeling, how they make meaning, and their worldview, you are more able to talk *to* them so they will hear you. Tailor your arguments to appeal to people's emotional needs and values directly.

- Any time we are presenting *any* kind of narrative to our listeners, we're telling a story. For good stories, relax, slow down, and keep things simple. **An interesting story = Subject + Captivating aspect about that subject.** Put your story into the format "Here's a topic and here's why it's interesting."

- Unless there is something genuinely new, interesting, captivating, unexpected, or emotionally relevant in a narrative we're sharing with someone, it's not going to hold their attention for very long. Be concise and find your unique angle. Keep in mind that what's "interesting" depends on your listener.

- Laughter serves many functions but is a primal "play signal" that communicates that things aren't so serious, there is no threat, and everyone is enjoying themselves. Laughter is a social lubricant. Humor is a mindset incompatible with taking yourself too seriously, a big ego, or anxiety. **Funny = (Normal + Absurd) Specificity.**

CHAPTER 4: ON HELPFUL BALANCES FOR PLEASING INTERACTIONS

- Dr. Gottman's "5:1 rule" suggests that **a healthy relationship follows the ratio of 5:1, with AT LEAST five positive interactions for every negative one.** This guideline reminds us that relationships need to be maintained over time.
- Criticism, defensiveness, contempt, and stonewalling are negative interactions, while positive interactions include support, validation, listening, affection, and so on. To counteract the negative effects of a single negative interaction during conflict, you need to consciously follow up with at least five positive interactions.
- Negative interactions are normal, but how you respond to them is your responsibility. Negative interactions are often much smaller and more subtle than this. There is no neutral—either an interaction helps rapport, or it hinders it.

- Charles Green's formula for trust is **Trustworthiness = (Credibility + Reliability + Intimacy) ÷ Self-Orientation**.
- Credibility relates to how believable and convincing they are (WORDS). Reliability refers to their ability to keep promises and fulfill the commitments they've made (ACTIONS). Intimacy involves the emotional aspect of trust, and the belief that personal values and boundaries will be respected (FEELINGS). Self-orientation refers to the person's focus, whether it is primarily on themselves or on others. Low self-orientation indicates a focus on others' needs and concerns, and leads to more trust.
- The highest possible score is thirty, but anything above eight or nine is pretty good. Remember also that trust is context dependent, and that too many unknowns often inspire mistrust.
- According to Roy Lewicki, the best apologies contain a few key elements, in order of importance: **acknowledgment of responsibility, offer to fix the problem, expression of regret, explanation of what went wrong, declaration of repentance, and a request for forgiveness**.
- Don't wait too long to apologize, don't over-apologize, and don't repeatedly apologize. Carefully match the apology to the person receiving it, the size of the offense, and the context.

CHAPTER 5: WHAT'S MY EXIT STRATEGY?

- Socially intelligent people don't experience less of this kind of conflict, they are simply better at managing it. The goal of assertive communication is to interact in such a way that both your rights and the other person's rights are respected. This ultimately preserves the relationship so that it can survive conflict/friction.

- Healthy communication is not passive (putting their needs first) or aggressive (putting your needs first) or passive aggressive (attempting to meet your needs in an underhanded way). Instead, it's clear, honest, direct, appropriate, polite, and respectful.

- The XYZ formula for assertive communication entails **X (the emotion you are feeling), Y (the specific behavior or action of the other person that is resulting in your emotion), and Z (the situation or context)**. End with a polite and reasonable request for the behavior you'd like.

- Avoid blaming, name-calling, or fruitless complaining. Calm compassion and clarity will go far to restoring harmony again.

- All conversations have a life cycle, and even good ones must end. To master the art of ending a conversation, include a content summary statement, a justification, a positive affect statement, a continuity statement, and some well-wishing to end.
- In words, that looks like, "Okay, we talked about what we needed to talk about [content summary statement], and I have a valid reason for ending our conversation [justification]. I enjoyed and appreciated our conversation [positive affect statement]. Let me reassure you that we will repeat it sometime in the future [continuity]. Take care, be happy, go well [well-wishing]."
- Err on the side of a shorter conversation rather than a longer one. If you are trapped in a "zombie conversation," then repeat the justification part again and more obviously, using nonverbal gestures and the actual word "goodbye." Ending relationships more generally can follow a similar format; always be kind and respectful.

Milton Keynes UK
Ingram Content Group UK Ltd.
UKHW010014020324
438794UK00003B/39

9 781647 435349